Body Music

Julie Maroh

BZZ
BZZ

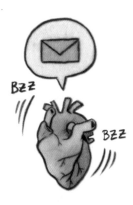

BODY MUSIC
by Julie Maroh
English-language translation copyright © 2017 by David Homel

First published in French as *Corps Sonores*
© Editions Glénat 2017

ARSENAL PULP PRESS
Suite 202 – 211 East Georgia St.
Vancouver, BC V6A 1Z6
Canada
arsenalpulp.com

This book has received support from the Institut français' Publication Support Programmes. Cet ouvrage a bénéficié du soutien des Programmes d'aide à la publication de l'Institut français.

Liberté · Égalité · Fraternité
RÉPUBLIQUE FRANÇAISE

The publisher gratefully acknowledges the support of the Government of Canada and the Government of British Columbia (through the Book Publishing Tax Credit Program) for its publishing activities.

Canada

Pages 6 to 9 contain words loosely inspired by "À chaque fois," words and music by Barbara

Editing of translation by Brian Lam
Design of translated edition by by Oliver McPartlin

Printed and bound in Canada

Library and Archives Canada Cataloguing in Publication:
Maroh, Julie, 1985-
[*Corps sonores*. English] Body music / Julie Maroh.

Translation of: *Corps sonores*.
Issued in print and electronic formats.
ISBN 978-1-55152-692-8 (softcover).—ISBN 978-1-55152-693-5 (HTML).
—ISBN 978-1-55152-694-2 (PDF)

1. Graphic novels. I. Title. II. Corps sonores. English

PN6747.M36C6713 2017   741.5'944   C2017-903946-6
                                                  C2017-903947-4

RUN THROUGH THE CHANNELS on the TV remote. The ads stream past; perfect skin, lustrous smiles.

Jump from station to station on your radio. A man announces he is looking for good car insurance, while his wife has found the detergent she was looking for. Double-click on your computer. The bodies are luscious, photo-shopped to within an inch of their lives; they say I do for ever and ever, he swears to stop watching porn, she promises to buy fewer pairs of shoes …

The daily dance of standards and stereotypes reminds us just how political the body is. The same is true of our love affairs. The image of the heterosexual, monogamous, white, handsome couple, with their toothpaste smiles for all eternity, stands in the collective unconscious as the ideal portrait of love. But where are the other realities? And where is mine?

Bow-legged, chubby, ethnic, androgynous, trans, pierced, scarred, ill, disabled, old, hairy, outside all the usual aesthetic criteria … Queers, dykes, trans, freaks, the non-monogamous, flighty and spiny hearts: we all write our own poems and our hearts beat harder for our romances. We are not a minority; we are the alternatives. There are as many love stories as there are imaginations.

This book is a sample of the palette. My toolbox may fall short when it comes to transcribing the taste of tears, or the terribly loud silence of a breaking heart, or the feel of skin rising in ecstatic waves. But I want this book to be an homage to all the loving beings who go against what is expected of them, sometimes risking their lives in the process.

These stories take place in Montreal, Canada, a place of multitudes.

The book begins on July 1, the date, in Montreal, when everything changes. It's moving day for many. Bodies load and unload trucks that each contain boxes and boxes of new emotions: hope, nostalgia, fear, doubt, excitement … In this organized chaos, in the sweltering heat, people leave behind the remains of their old lives on the sidewalks and take only what matters, on their way toward creating new ones.

—Julie Maroh

MONTREAL, JULY 1ST

Whenever people talk about love

It's always "never" and "always"

Listen, I swear ...

... that before you there was nothing ...

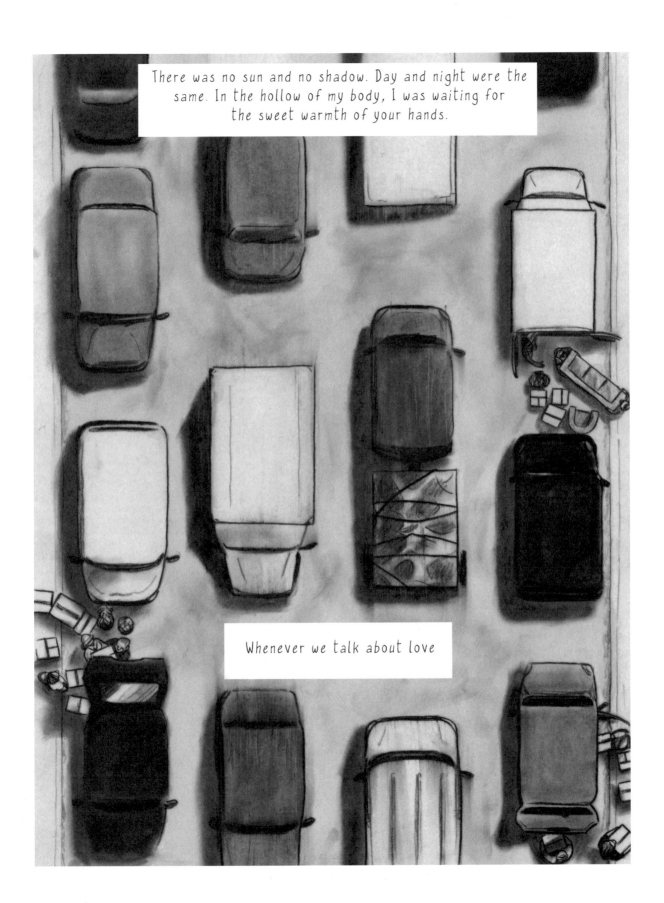

There was no sun and no shadow. Day and night were the same. In the hollow of my body, I was waiting for the sweet warmth of your hands.

Whenever we talk about love

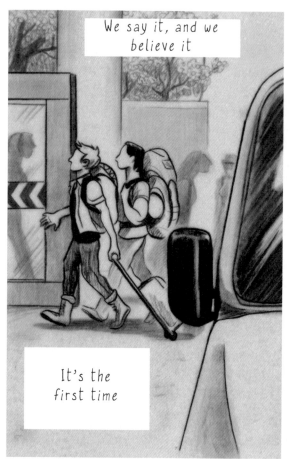

We say it, and we believe it

It's the first time

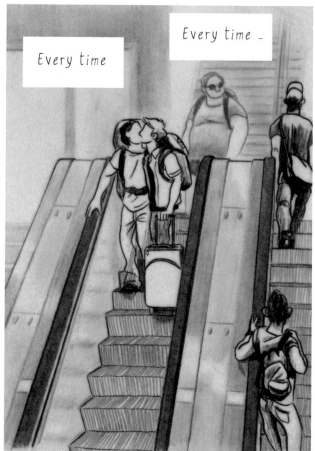

Every time

Every time ...

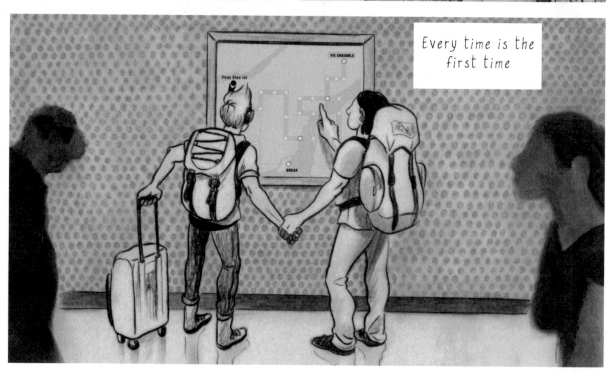

Every time is the first time

If only we could, each time
Love and lie about love
LIFE TOGETHER
You are here
MEETING
BREAK-UP
BREAK-OFF
Like every time
Like each time
Like every time

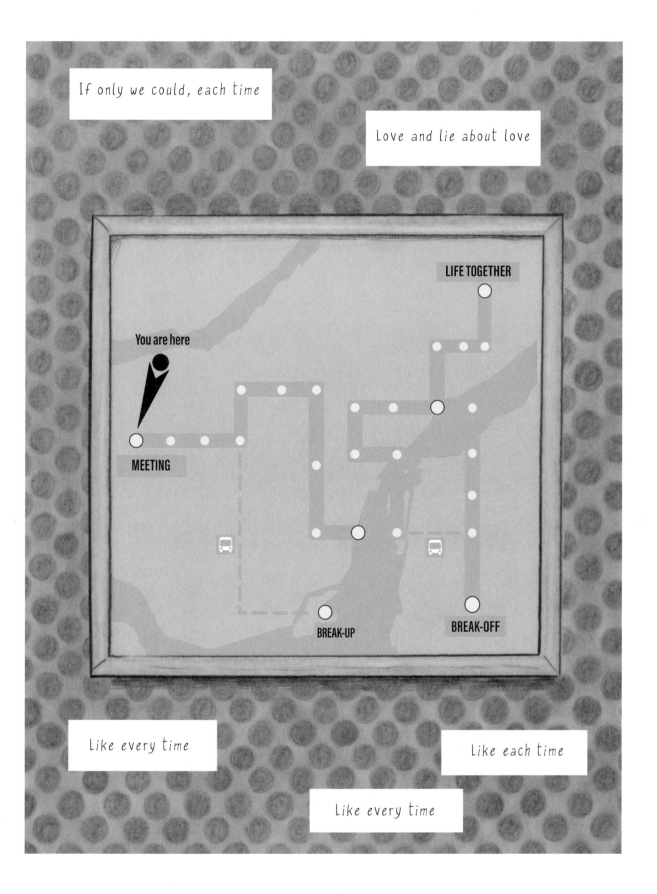

1.

Looking out the Window
on rue Boyer

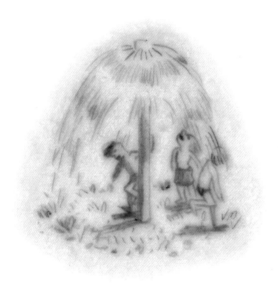

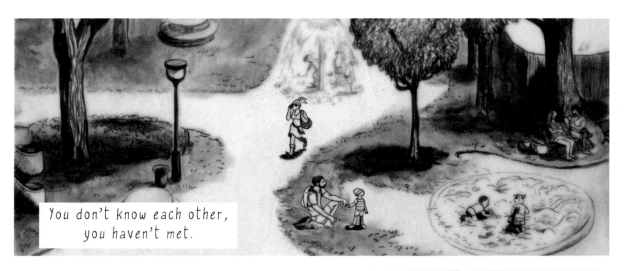

You don't know each other, you haven't met.

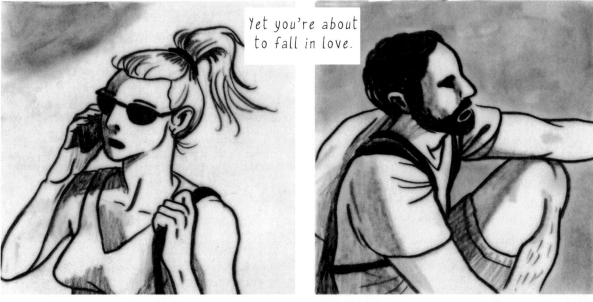

Yet you're about to fall in love.

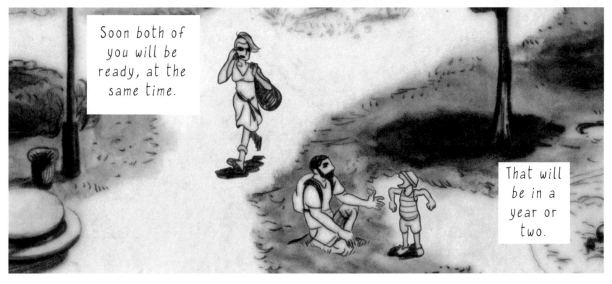

Soon both of you will be ready, at the same time.

That will be in a year or two.

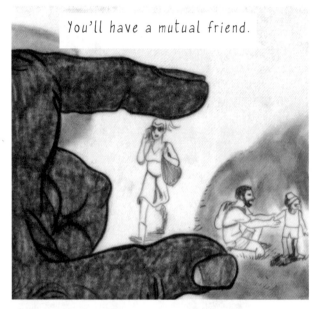

You'll have a mutual friend.

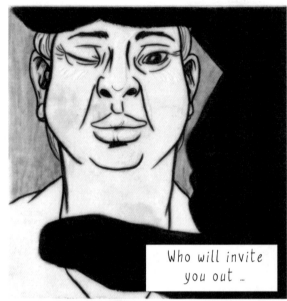

Who will invite you out ...

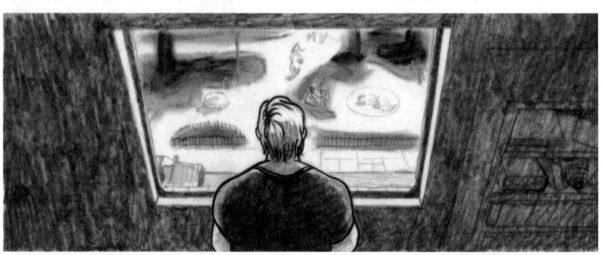

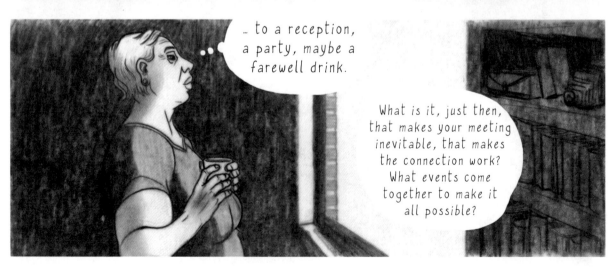

... to a reception, a party, maybe a farewell drink.

What is it, just then, that makes your meeting inevitable, that makes the connection work? What events come together to make it all possible?

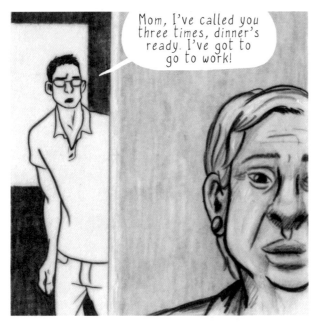

Mom, I've called you three times, dinner's ready. I've got to go to work!

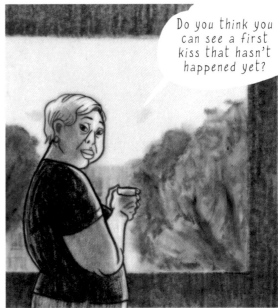

Do you think you can see a first kiss that hasn't happened yet?

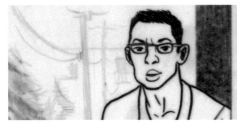

Come on, cut the nonsense! It's time to eat.

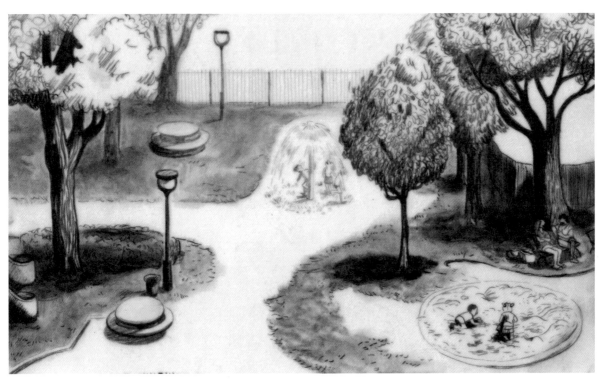

2.

The Encounter

YEAH
HIGH FIVE
WAY TO GO!

ALL RIGHT!

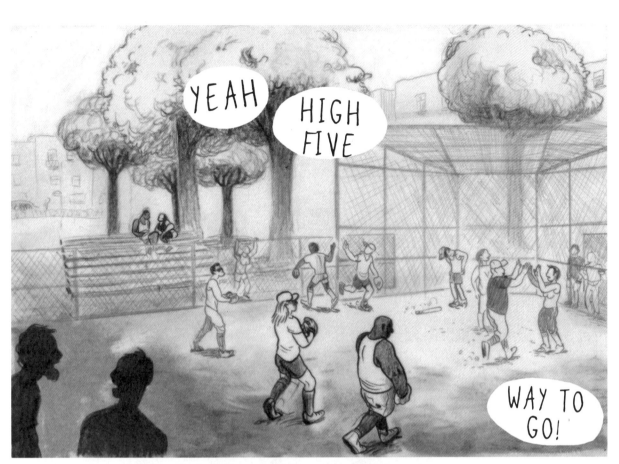

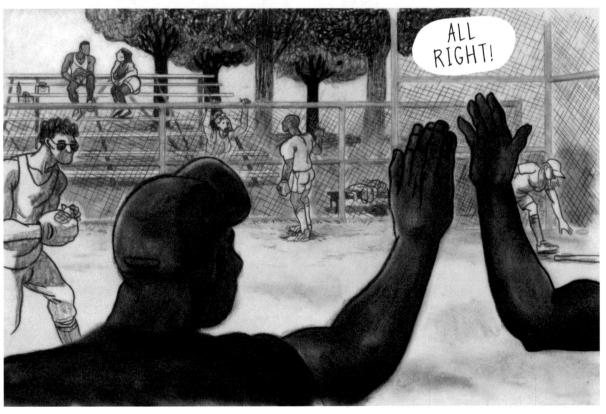

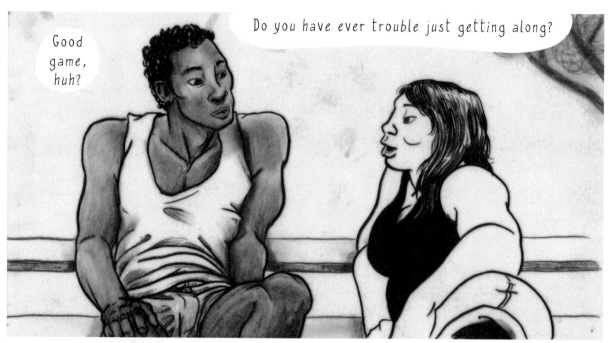

Good game, huh?

Do you have ever trouble just getting along?

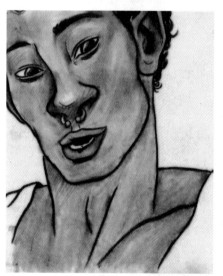

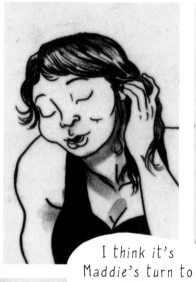

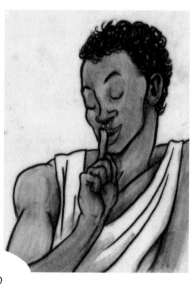

I think it's Maddie's turn to bat!

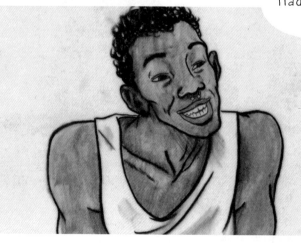

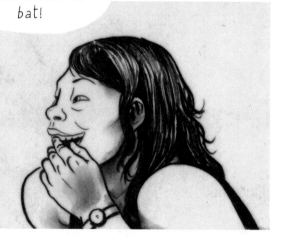

I know what you mean.
GO! GO! GO!
Go-o-o! All the way!
Holy shit!
Any beer left?
What about Ahmed?
I think he's playing another game!

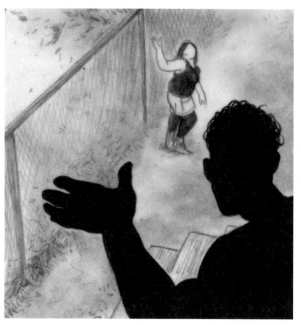

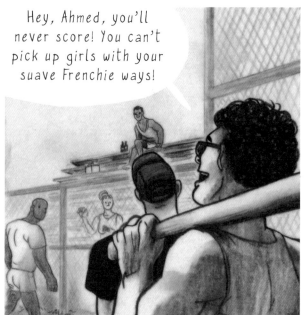

Hey, Ahmed, you'll never score! You can't pick up girls with your suave Frenchie ways!

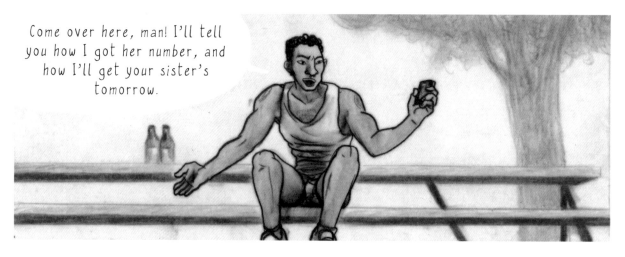

Come over here, man! I'll tell you how I got her number, and how I'll get your sister's tomorrow.

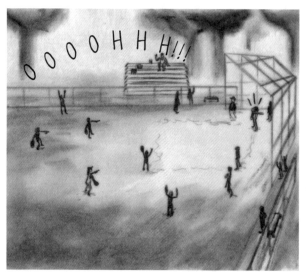

OOOOHHH!!!

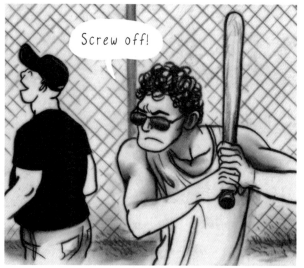

Screw off!

3.

"Are you sure you want to delete this contact?"

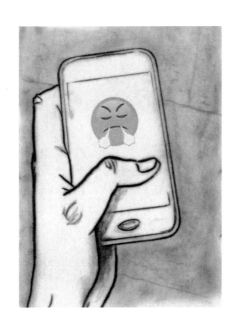

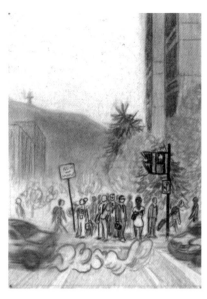

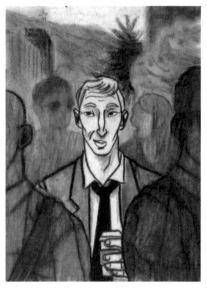

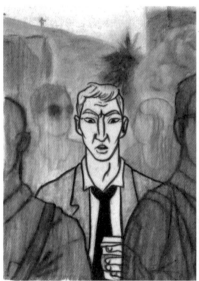

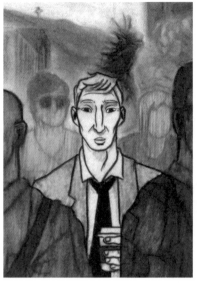

Cut it out with your stupid questions!

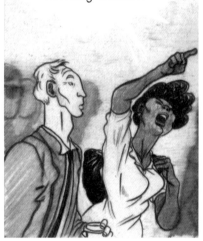

The light's red, you fucking maniac!

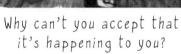

Why can't you accept that it's happening to you?

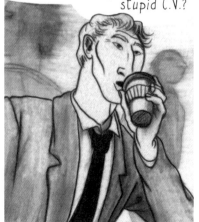

The guy's fun, smart, good-looking … Who cares if he's an Anglo and has a stupid C.V.?

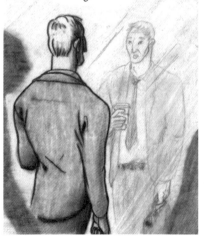

He's your type, right?

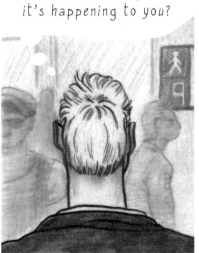

27

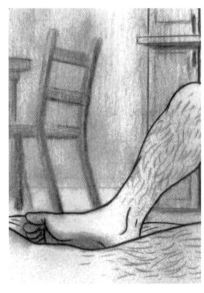
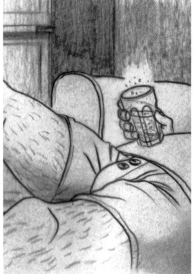
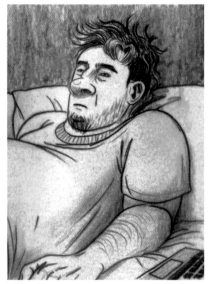

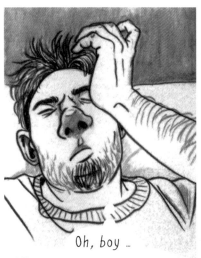

Oh, boy ...
Who made me drink so much?

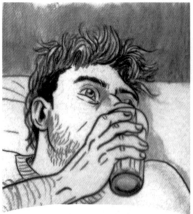

Were you trying to impress him, or have the worst first date in the world?

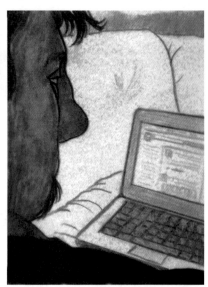

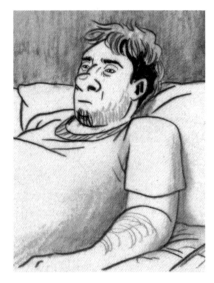

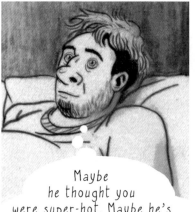

Maybe he thought you were super-hot. Maybe he's dreaming of you and trying to find the right words to ask you for another date.

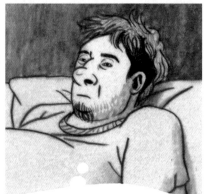

But really, am I going to lose my head over a guy who's 15 years older?

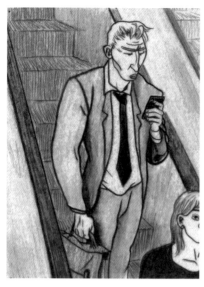

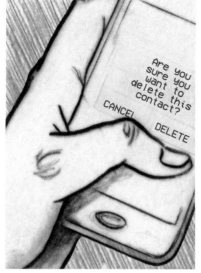

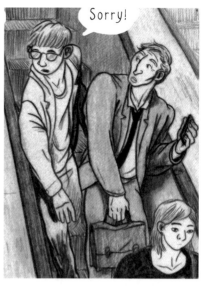

Sorry!

You stupid fool ... You're trying to make his faults worse to cover your own cowardice.

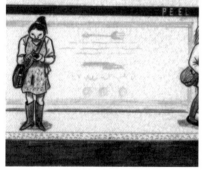

So why'd you stalk him on that dumb-ass dating site and invite him to dinner?

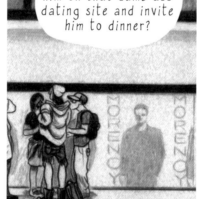

Then you didn't kiss him when you should have ...

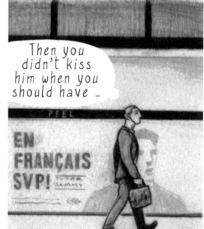

Everyone in the bar could smell his whisky breath, he was that drunk.

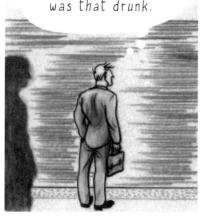

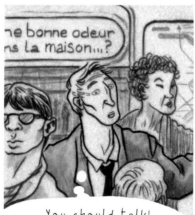

You should talk! All you could do was stare at his eyes and mouth.

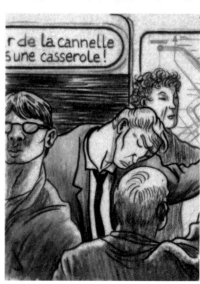

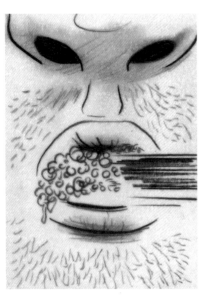

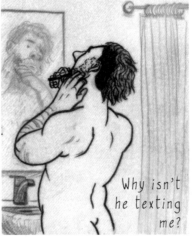

Yeah, but when he did that, what did it really mean?

Why isn't he texting me?

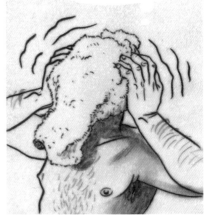

He said he would, so I can't do it first, that would screw everything up.

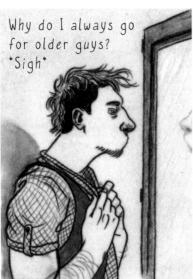

Why do I always go for older guys? *Sigh*

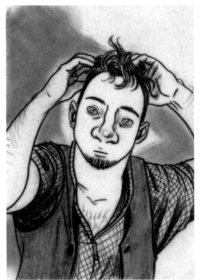

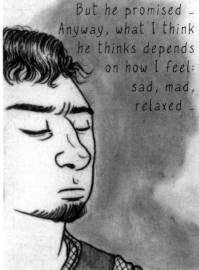

But he promised ... Anyway, what I think he thinks depends on how I feel: sad, mad, relaxed ...

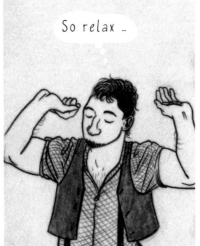

So relax ...

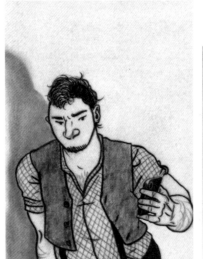

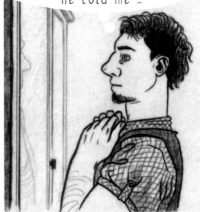

What made me want to kiss him? When I said, "Were you brought up in a barn?" and he told me ...

30

"Yeah, the same barn we were all brought up in."

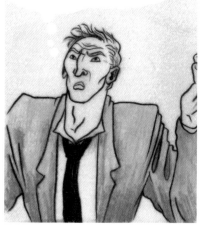

Do you always have to moralize with everybody?

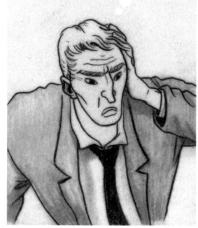

He was being smart and you had to be smarter?

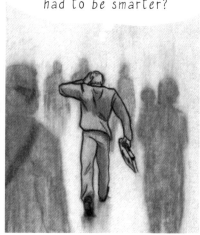

Maybe he talked about his C.V. and his job in that pushy way for the same reason some guys buy a big SUV ...

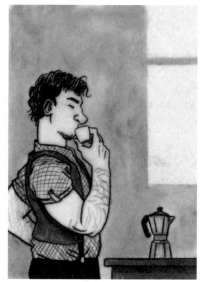

To make up for having a little dick?

DO YOU SPEAK ENGLISH?!

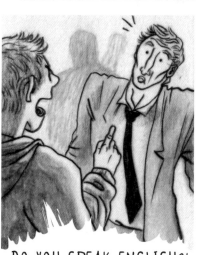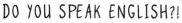

The English were here first, this is fucking Canada, we speak English!

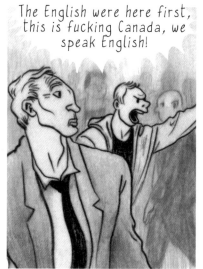

What does he think about French people like me?

31

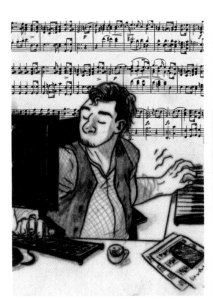

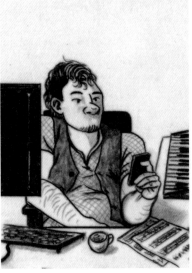

Whatever.

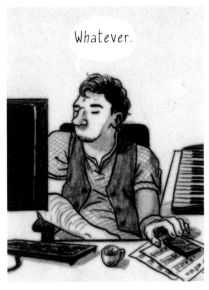

No, no, you're just too stupid!

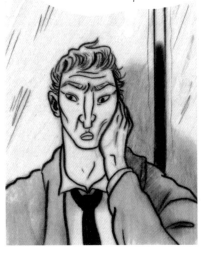

Why would he want to see you again? Who can stand you?

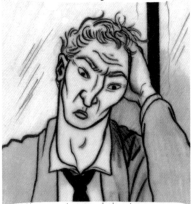

Who would want to be your boyfriend, huh?

He'll tell you to take a walk. Spare yourself the humiliation...

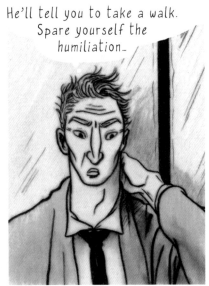

Sigh

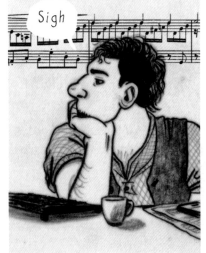

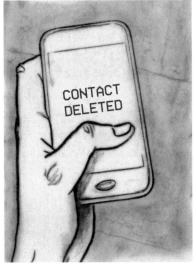

CONTACT DELETED

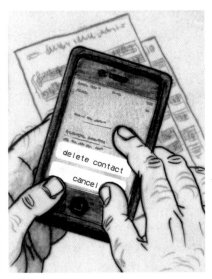

delete contact

cancel

4.

Playing with Fire

Thank you for joining us. Hélène will now sign copies of her book for those who would like one.

Bonjour
Bonjour. Tu es anglo-phone?
Yes. I'm from London.
We can speak English if you like.
I'd be glad to. My name is Gemma.
Pleased to meet you.
Where are you from?
Mexico. Mixed background.
I'm from Martinique.
I know.

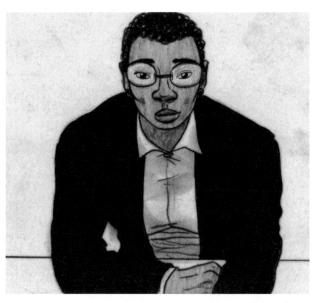
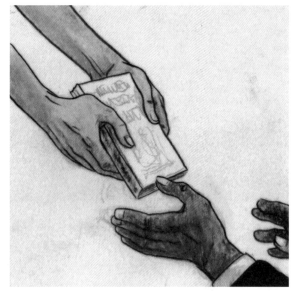

Yes, well ... What are you doing in Montreal?

Research?

I'm a journalist and a writer. I'm doing research here.

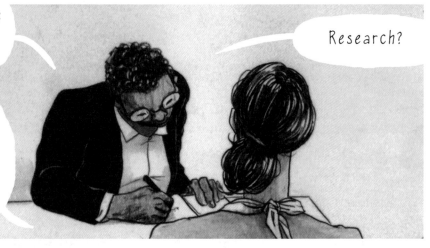

If you're curious, why don't we talk about it over dinner?

I reserved a table at the hotel.

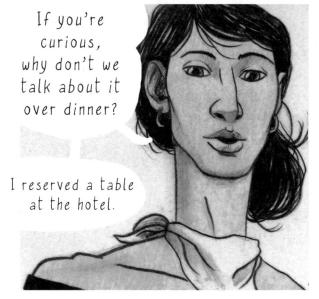
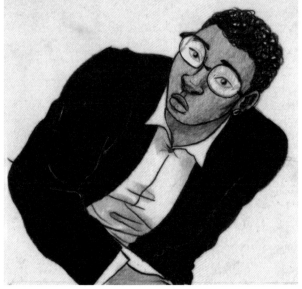

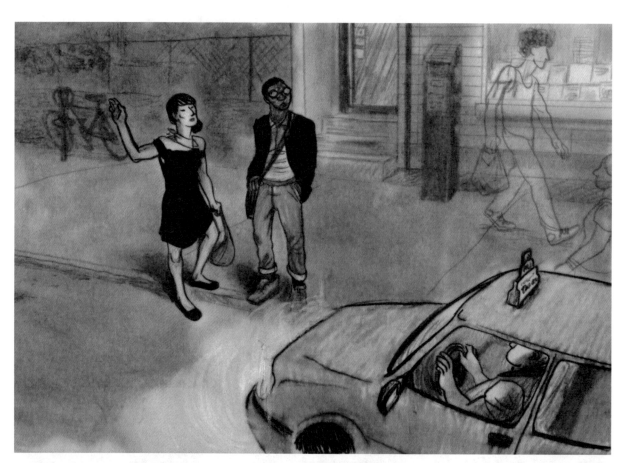

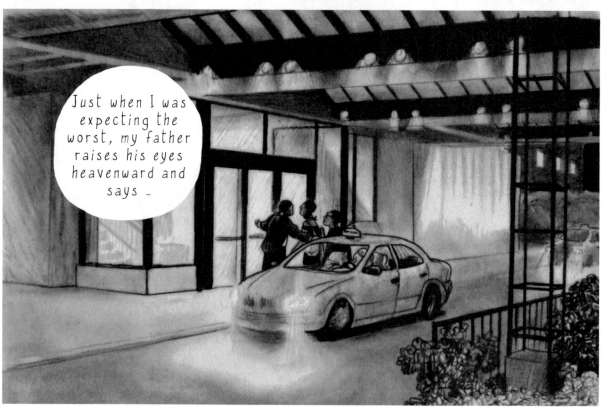

Just when I was expecting the worst, my father raises his eyes heavenward and says …

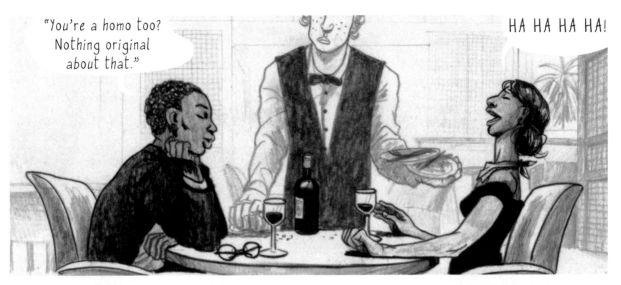

"You're a homo too? Nothing original about that."

HA HA HA HA!

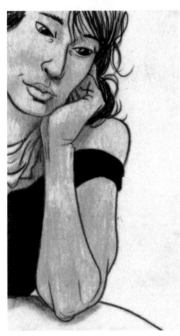

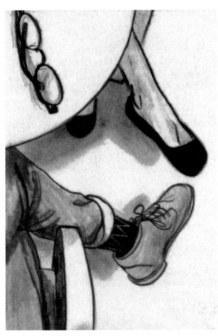

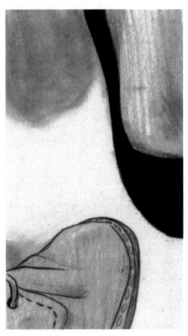

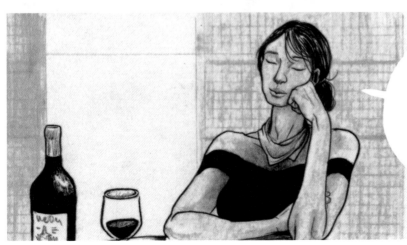

This is such lovely torture. I'm dying to caress your foot with mine.

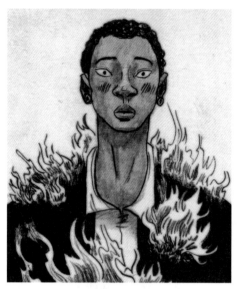

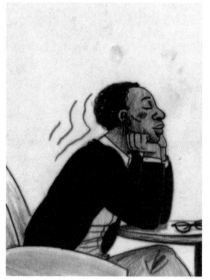

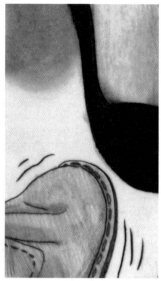

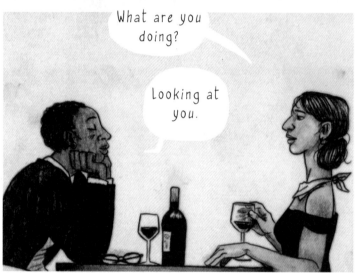

What are you doing?

Looking at you.

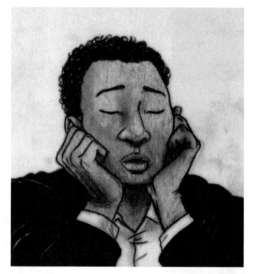

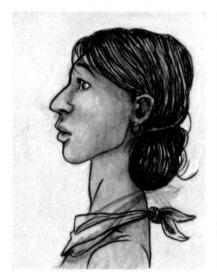

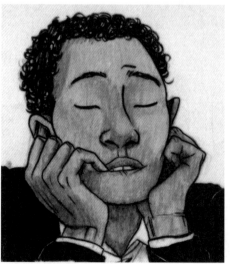

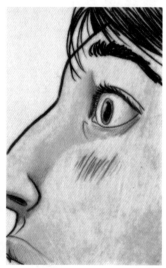

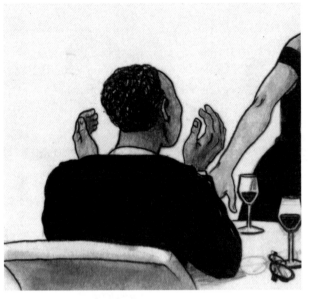
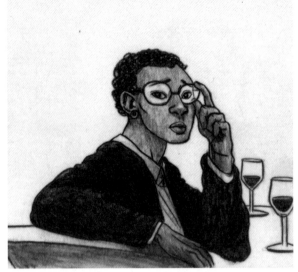
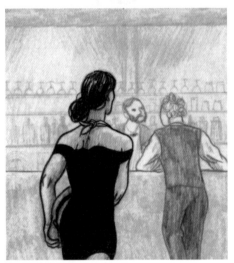
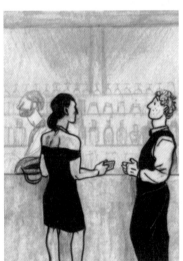
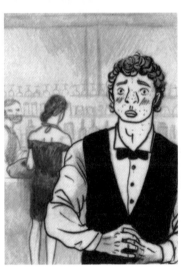
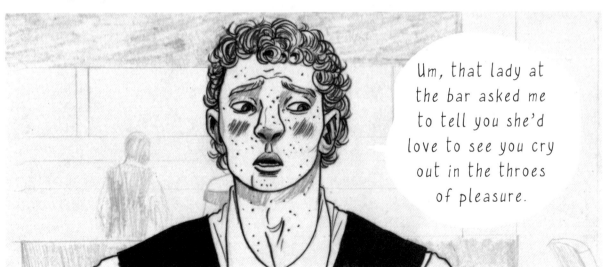

Um, that lady at the bar asked me to tell you she'd love to see you cry out in the throes of pleasure.

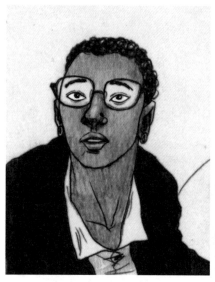

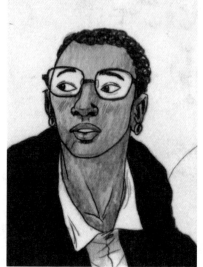

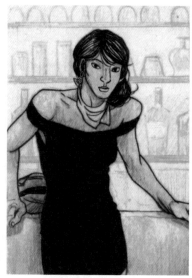

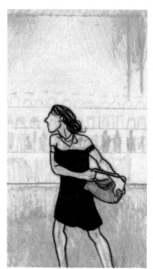

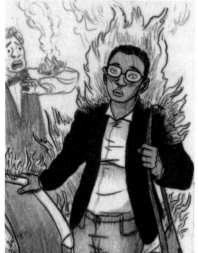

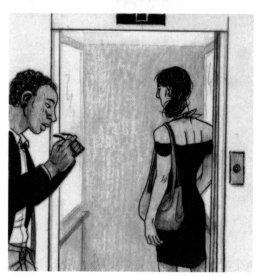

You brought me here on purpose …

You have a room here, right?

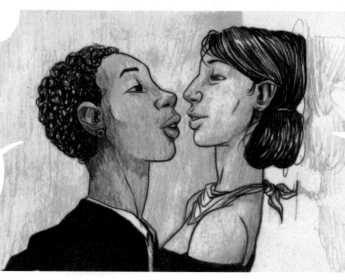

Do I have such a terrible accent in French?

5.

What Do We Do with Last's Night's Passion?

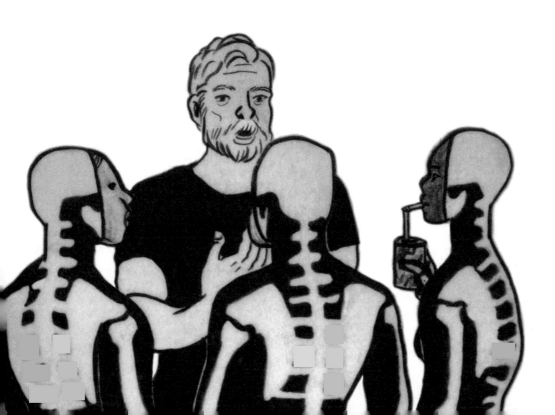

Hurry up, guys!

When Guy Maddin finishes his interview, we'll start up again.
Ok
Hey … am I hallucinating, or are you wearing the same outfit you had on yesterday? And your face is a mess! You slept in a different bed last night and forgot to look in the mirror this morning, ha ha!
I'll go get the water bottles for the actors.

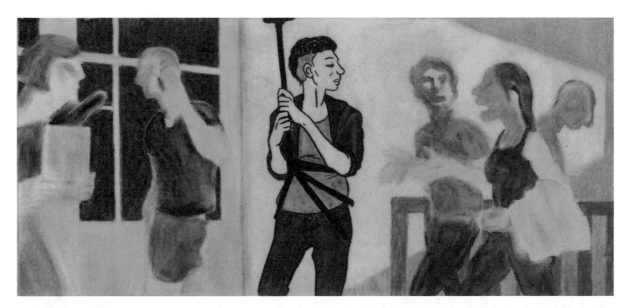

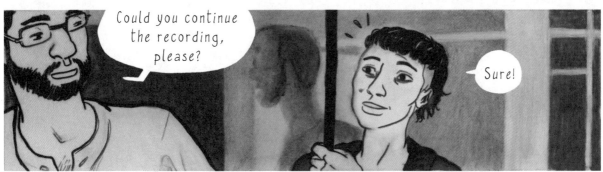

Could you continue the recording, please?

Sure!

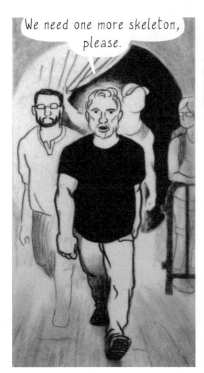

We need one more skeleton, please.

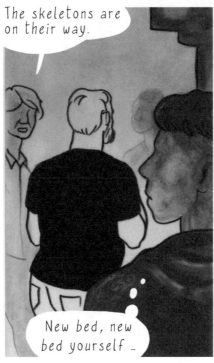

The skeletons are on their way.

New bed, new bed yourself ...

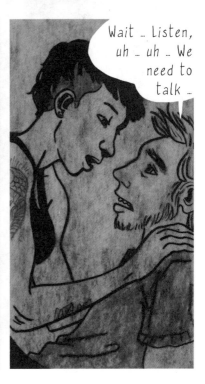

Wait ... Listen, uh ... uh ... We need to talk ...

What, like, right NOW?
I'm trans.
It's funny when you think about it … I generally identify as a lesbian. Normally I don't go for guys. But I felt like a guy myself when I was coming on to him …

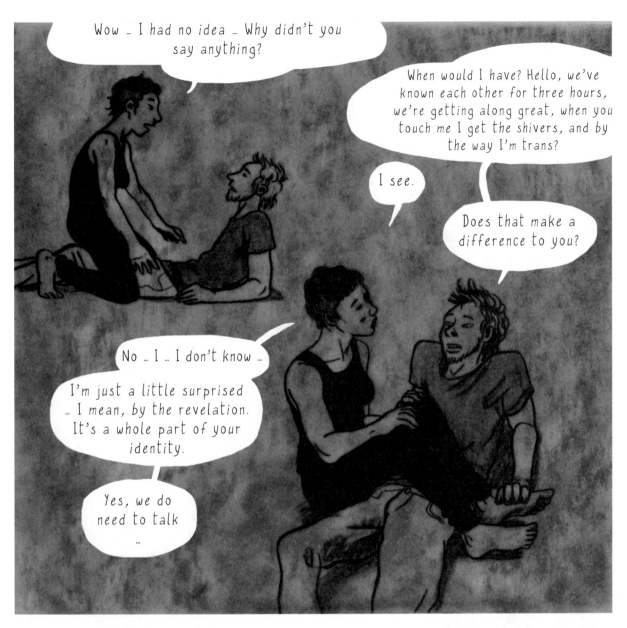

Wow ... I had no idea ... Why didn't you say anything?

When would I have? Hello, we've known each other for three hours, we're getting along great, when you touch me I get the shivers, and by the way I'm trans?

I see.

Does that make a difference to you?

No ... I ... I don't know ...

I'm just a little surprised ... I mean, by the revelation. It's a whole part of your identity.

Yes, we do need to talk ...

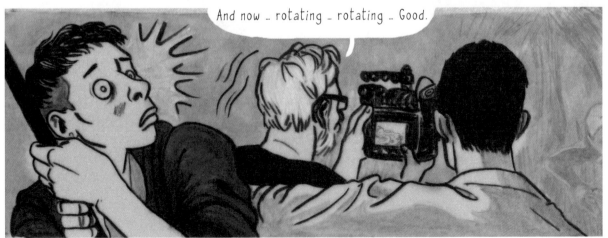

And now ... rotating ... rotating ... Good.

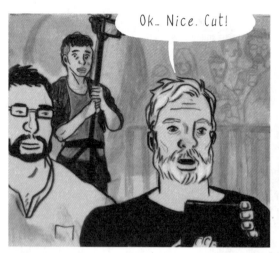

Ok… Nice. Cut!

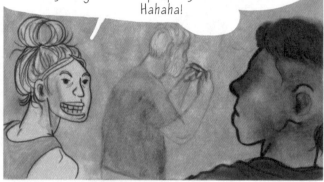

Hey, did you get any sleep at all? That reminds me of the night you drank too much and went staggering down the street, shouting "Nothing means anything more than anything else!" to people you'd never met. Hahaha!

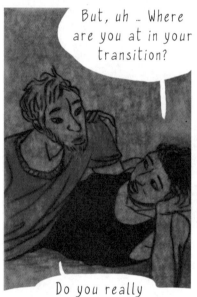

But, uh … Where are you at in your transition?

Do you really need those details now?

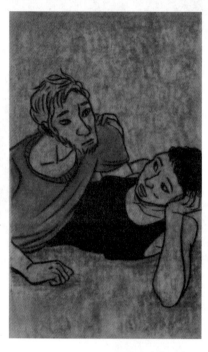

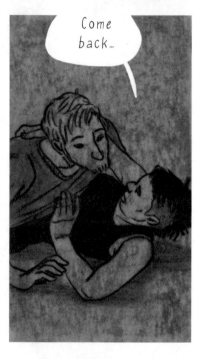

Come back…

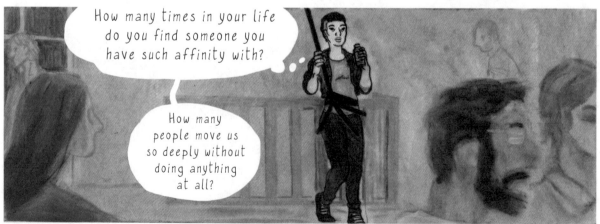

How many times in your life do you find someone you have such affinity with?

How many people move us so deeply without doing anything at all?

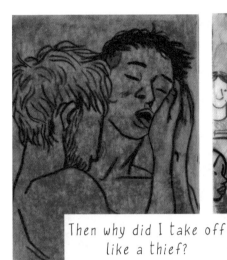

Then why did I take off
like a thief?

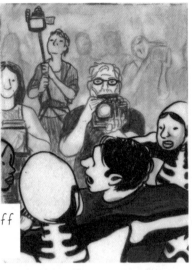

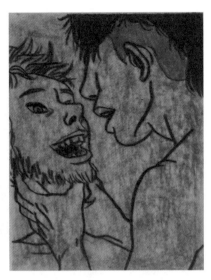

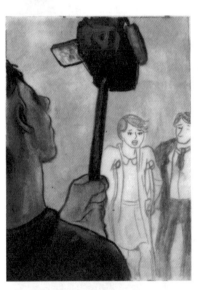

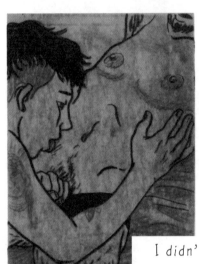

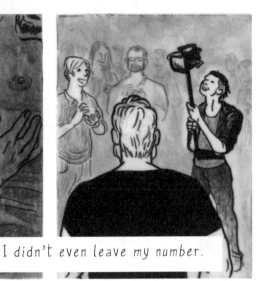

I didn't even leave my number.

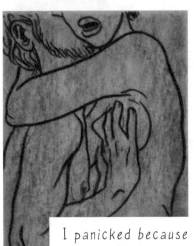

I panicked because he's trans and socially, it
would be worse than being a lesbian.

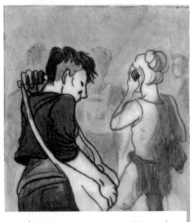

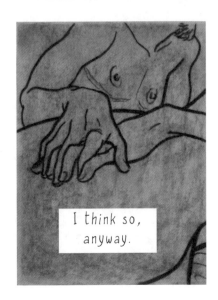

I think so,
anyway.

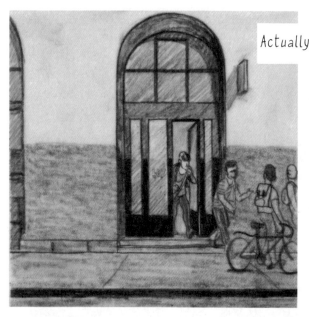

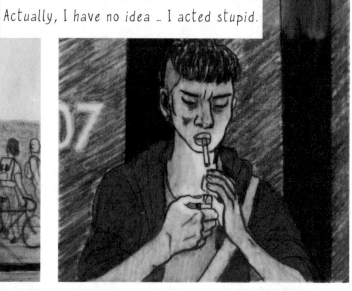

Actually, I have no idea ... I acted stupid.

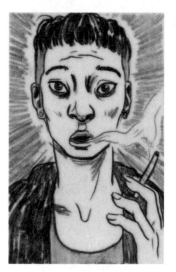

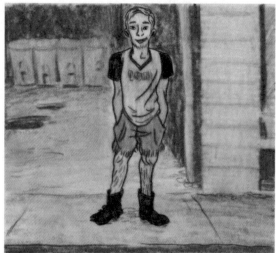

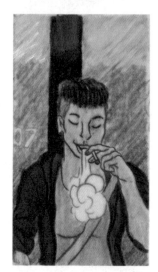

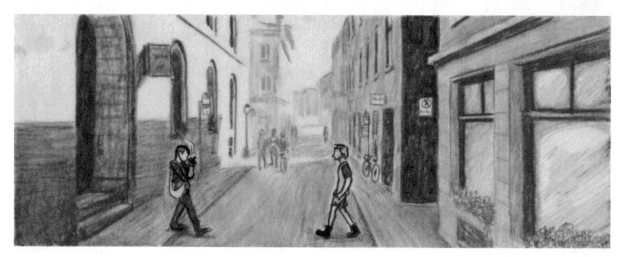

You should never tell a stranger where you work.
Still, you can't help satisfying people's fascination for sordid news items and bad fiction.

Madame's carriage is ready!
Would Madame care to go for a drink?

6.

Fantasies of the Hypothetical

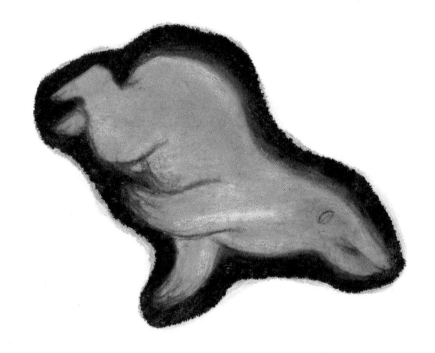

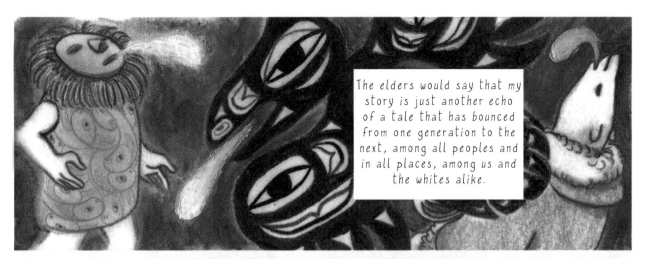

The elders would say that my story is just another echo of a tale that has bounced from one generation to the next, among all peoples and in all places, among us and the whites alike.

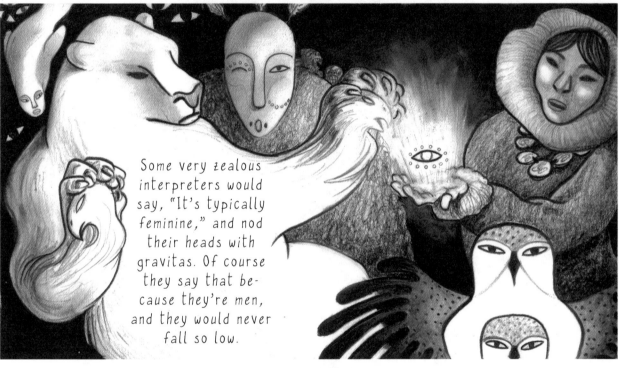

Some very zealous interpreters would say, "It's typically feminine," and nod their heads with gravitas. Of course they say that because they're men, and they would never fall so low.

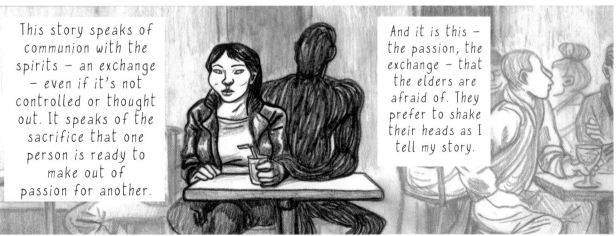

This story speaks of communion with the spirits – an exchange – even if it's not controlled or thought out. It speaks of the sacrifice that one person is ready to make out of passion for another.

And it is this – the passion, the exchange – that the elders are afraid of. They prefer to shake their heads as I tell my story.

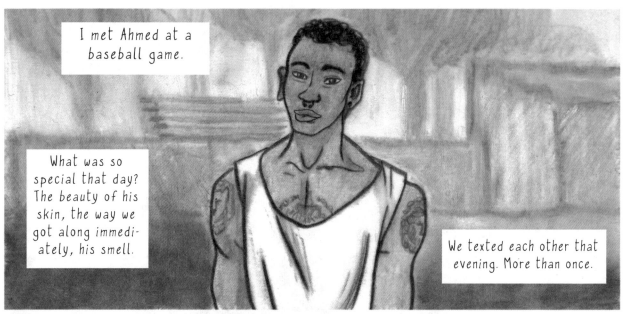

I met Ahmed at a baseball game.

What was so special that day? The beauty of his skin, the way we got along immediately, his smell.

We texted each other that evening. More than once.

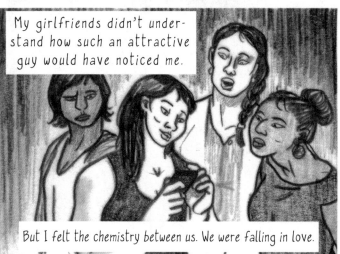

My girlfriends didn't understand how such an attractive guy would have noticed me.

But I felt the chemistry between us. We were falling in love.

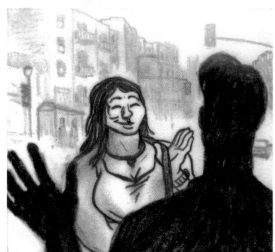

We met soon after. We spent the day together, without a moment apart, and then, I don't remember what the excuse was, we ended up at my place and we just devoured each other.

With endless hunger.

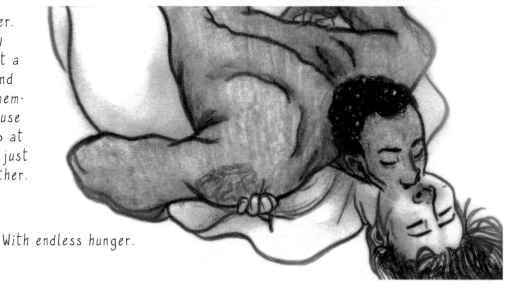

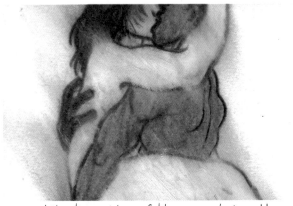

Like two sides of the same being. We didn't waste time sleeping.

He left the next morning ... He had to work. He was so beautiful.

I've been waiting ever since.

We were supposed to see each other again. He had to cancel more than once, he was sorry, his messages were full of tenderness ...

Then he stopped answering. Six days ago.

At first, I went out. I saw my girlfriends. They couldn't believe we'd slept together. They had that surprised and envious look, and I was proud. I felt so in love and missed him so much. I could have eaten him alive.

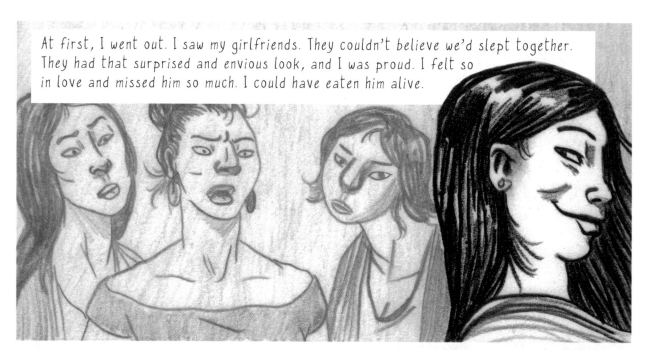

Then one morning, sadness kept me from getting out of bed. I was afraid ... Maybe my friends were right? No, that couldn't be.

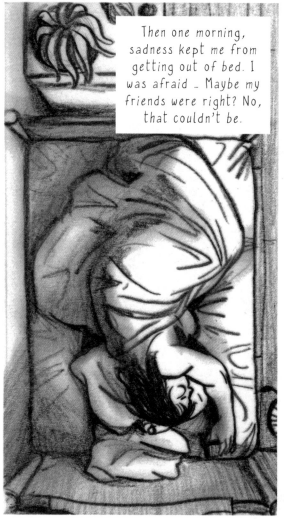

I went on waiting.

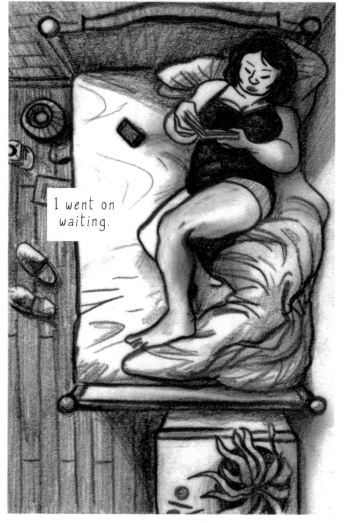

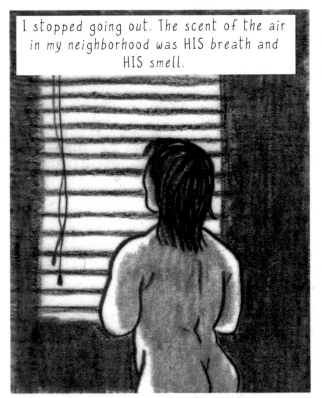

I stopped going out. The scent of the air in my neighborhood was HIS breath and HIS smell.

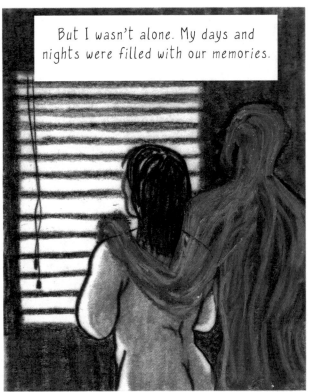

But I wasn't alone. My days and nights were filled with our memories.

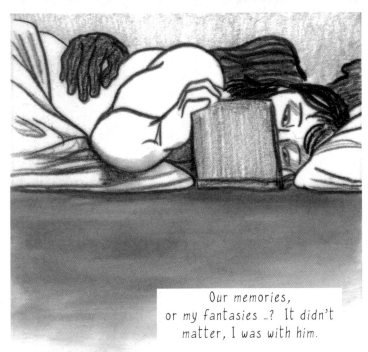

Our memories, or my fantasies ...? It didn't matter, I was with him.

In my belly I felt the storm of desire rise up, my blood coursing and my heart racing.

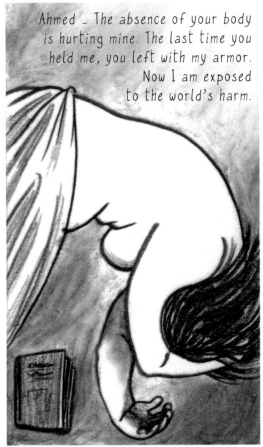

Ahmed ... The absence of your body is hurting mine. The last time you held me, you left with my armor. Now I am exposed to the world's harm.

I started to receive visits, hauntings.
Was it because of hunger? Or the moon's cycle?
I felt the spirits whirling around me.
I recognized them but couldn't remember their names.
Why had they come? Had I called upon them?

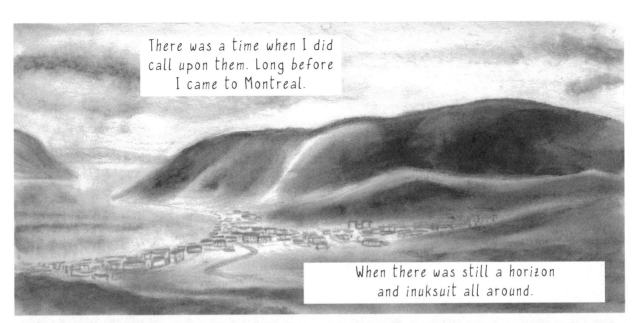

There was a time when I did call upon them. Long before I came to Montreal.

When there was still a horizon and inuksuit all around.

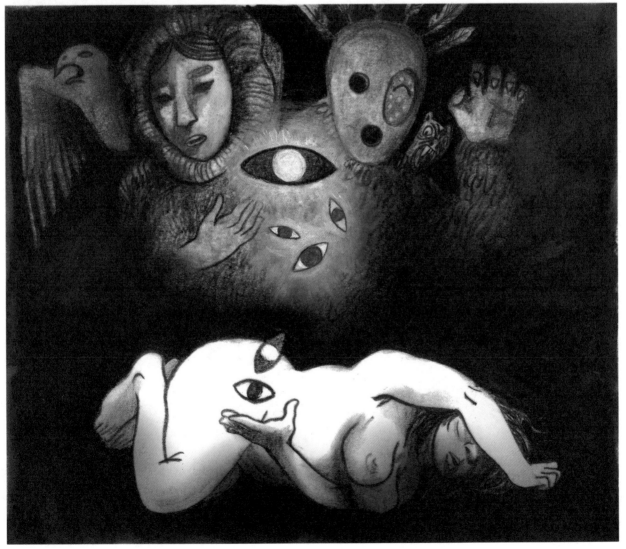

69

I've slept deeply these last few days ... I have a vague memory of the spirits ... an exchange.

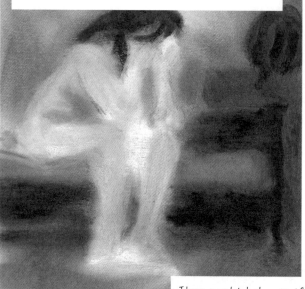

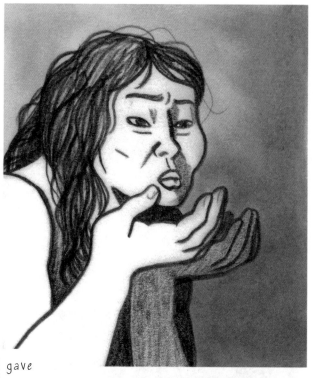

They would help me if I gave them something in return. I had slept too much ... My vision was blurry. The colors seemed to fade.

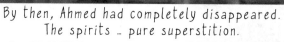

By then, Ahmed had completely disappeared. The spirits ... pure superstition.

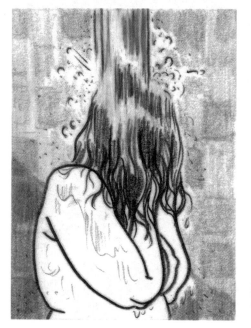

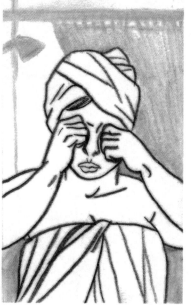

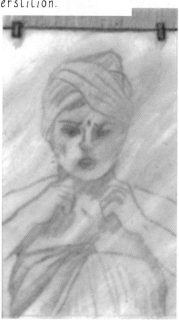

Day after day I lay prostrate in half-sleep, in love as ever, thinking back.

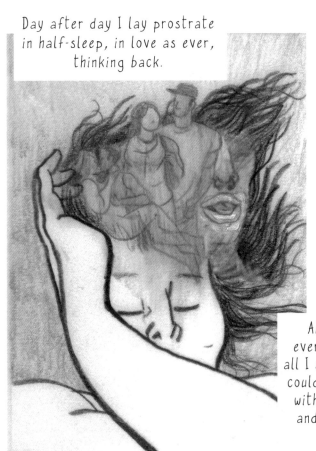

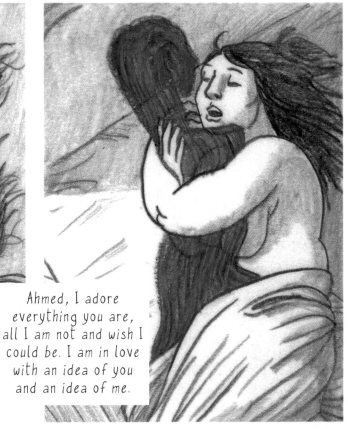

Ahmed, I adore everything you are, all I am not and wish I could be. I am in love with an idea of you and an idea of me.

When did we see each other? Last month ...? What really happened and what have I imagined since then? Every day I relive the fantasy of how we might meet again.

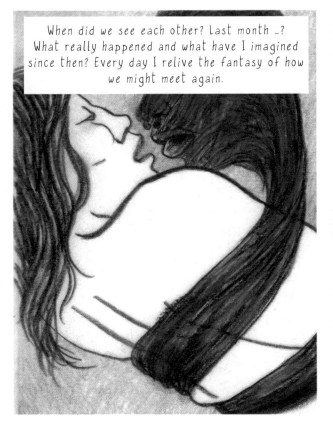

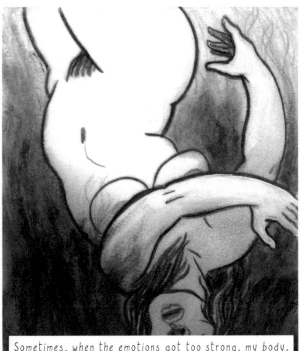

Sometimes, when the emotions got too strong, my body, deprived of nourishment, would defend itself, and make me lose consciousness. Every time I woke up, my vision was more blurred, and colors started to fade.

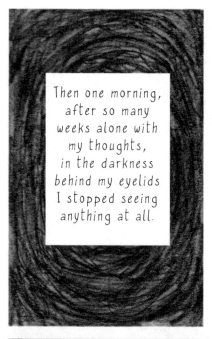

Then one morning, after so many weeks alone with my thoughts, in the darkness behind my eyelids I stopped seeing anything at all.

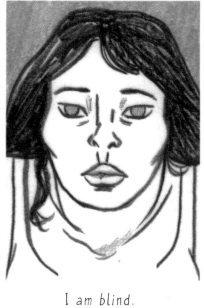

I am blind.

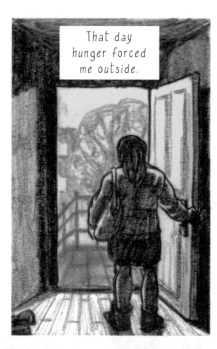

That day hunger forced me outside.

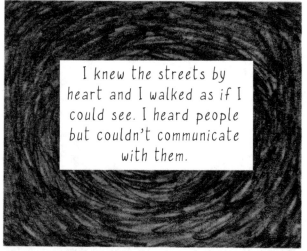

I knew the streets by heart and I walked as if I could see. I heard people but couldn't communicate with them.

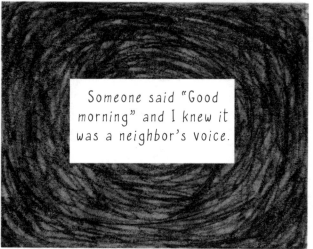

Someone said "Good morning" and I knew it was a neighbor's voice.

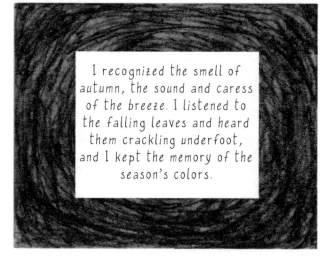

I recognized the smell of autumn, the sound and caress of the breeze. I listened to the falling leaves and heard them crackling underfoot, and I kept the memory of the season's colors.

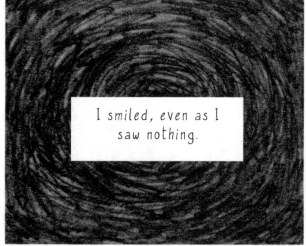

I smiled, even as I saw nothing.

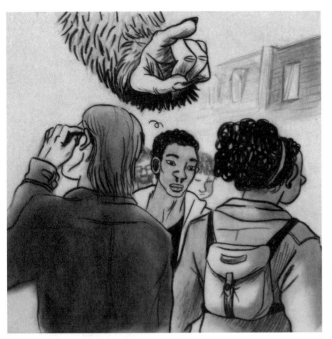
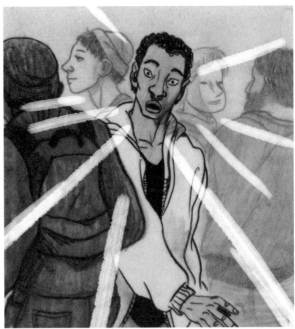
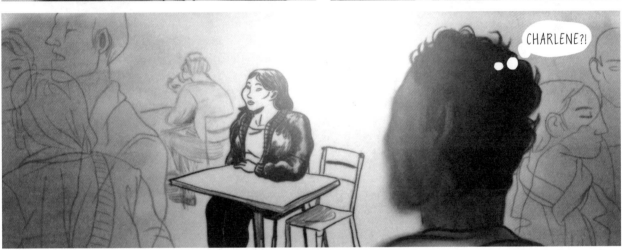

CHARLENE?!

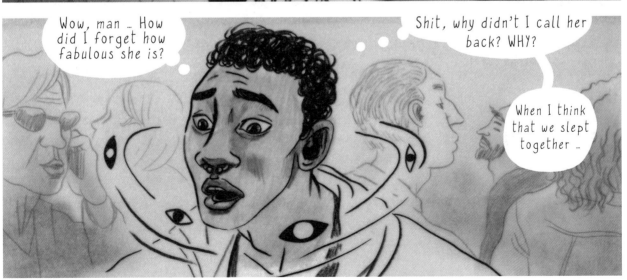

Wow, man ... How did I forget how fabulous she is?

Shit, why didn't I call her back? WHY?

When I think that we slept together ...

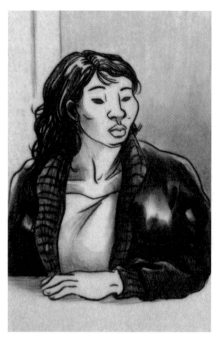
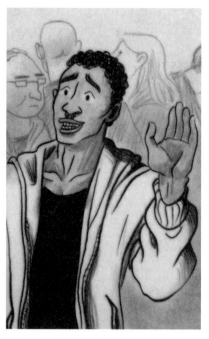
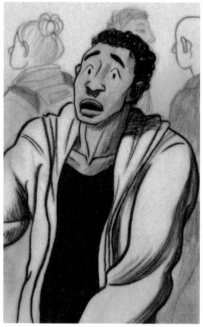
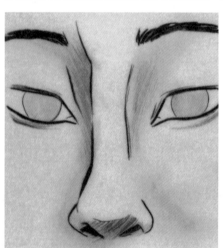
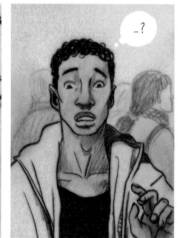
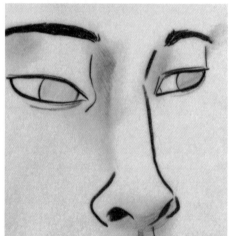
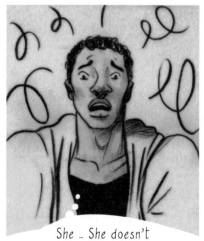

She ... She doesn't
recognize me or she's ignoring me?
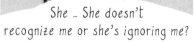

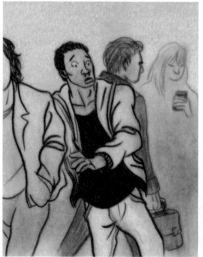
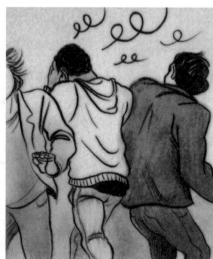

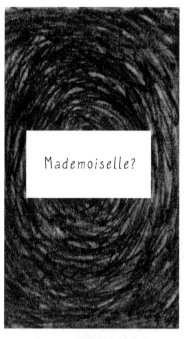

Mademoiselle?

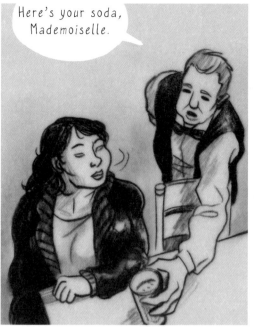

Here's your soda, Mademoiselle.

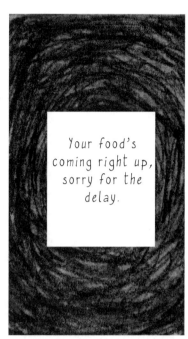

Your food's coming right up, sorry for the delay.

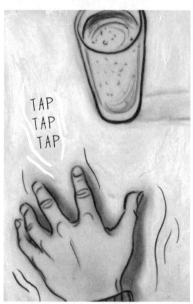

TAP
TAP
TAP

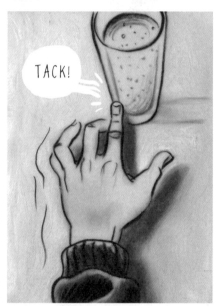

TACK!

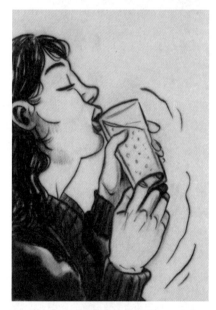

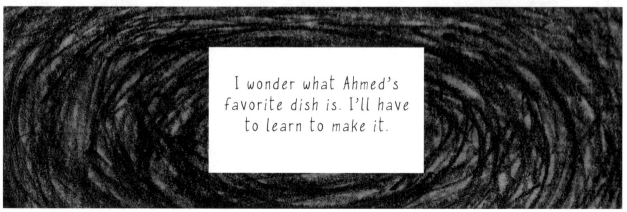

I wonder what Ahmed's favorite dish is. I'll have to learn to make it.

7.

Polyamorous Love and Friendship

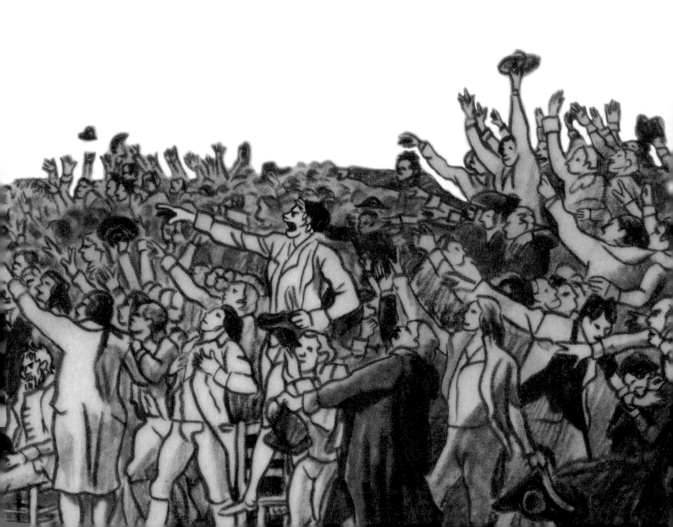

RRR
VRRRR
VRRR
CRR
CRAC
RRR
RRRR
VRR
VRR

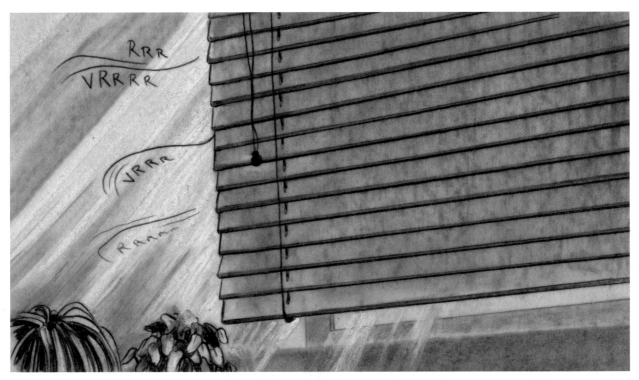

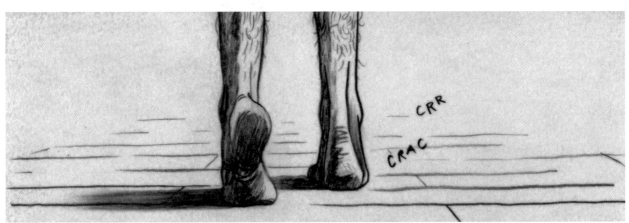

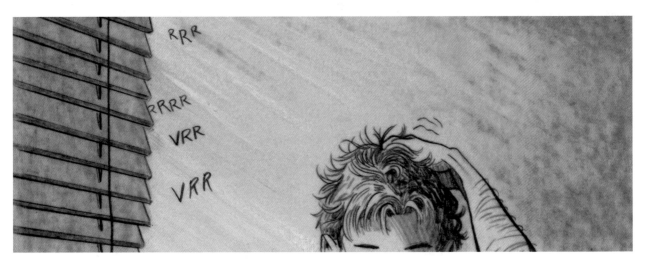

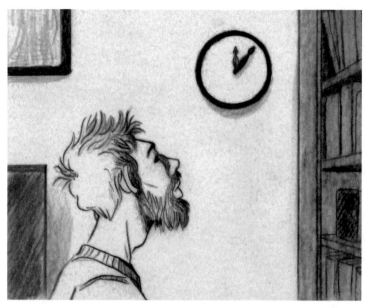

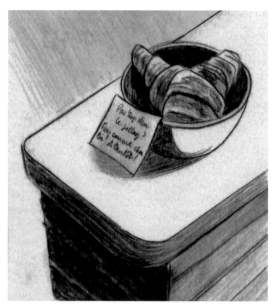

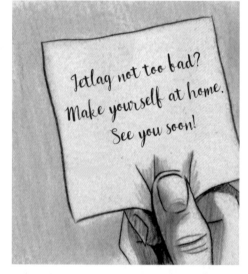

Jetlag not too bad?
Make yourself at home.
See you soon!

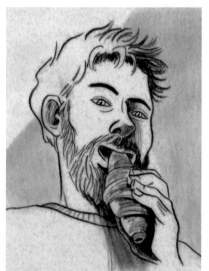

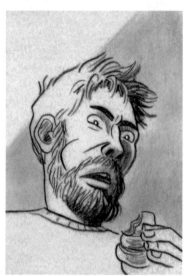

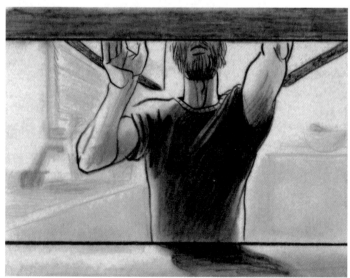

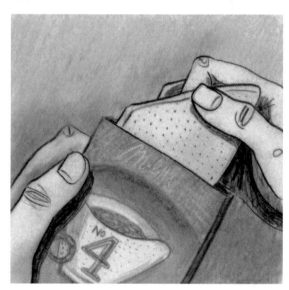

GRRCRCR
CRRRR

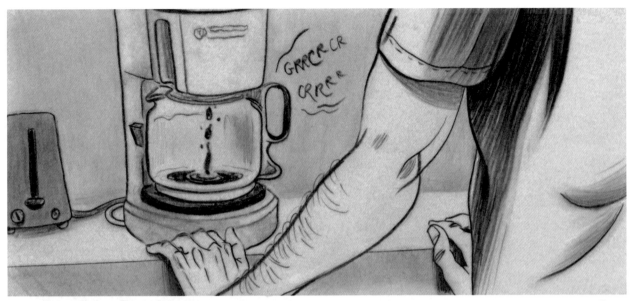

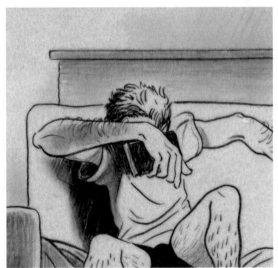

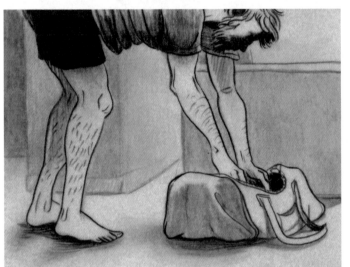

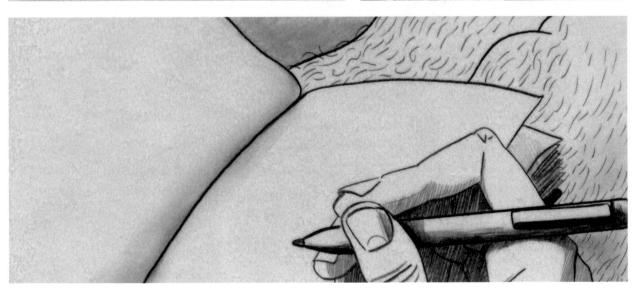

Touchdown in Montreal this evening in the sweet-ness of Indian summer.
VRRR
RRR
VRR
RRR
GRR
My friends are a second family. We get closer with every trip.

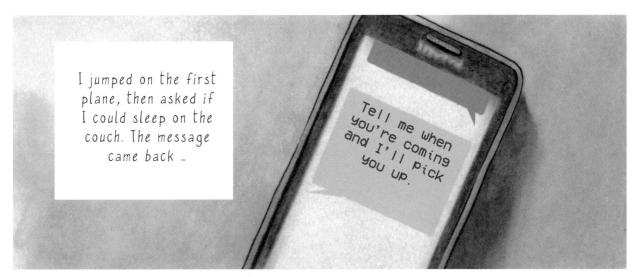

I jumped on the first plane, then asked if I could sleep on the couch. The message came back ...

Tell me when you're coming and I'll pick you up.

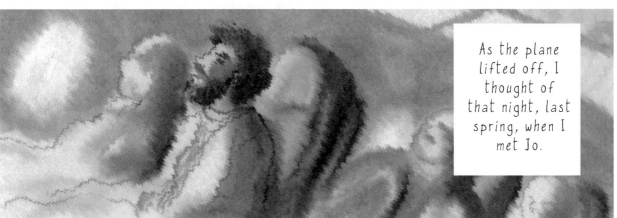

As the plane lifted off, I thought of that night, last spring, when I met Jo.

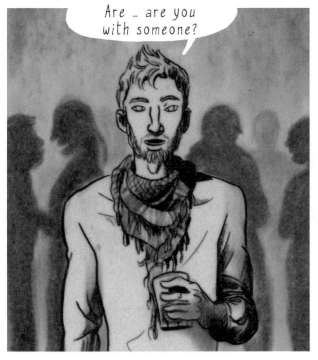

Are ... are you with someone?

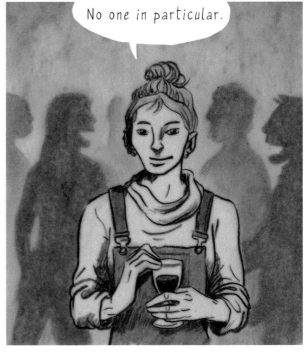

No one in particular.

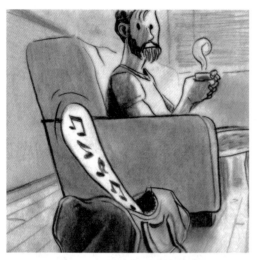

You get any sleep?

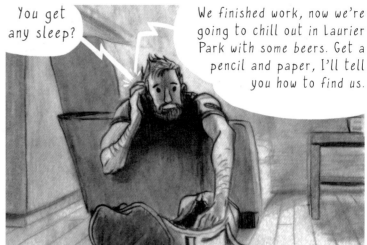

We finished work, now we're going to chill out in Laurier Park with some beers. Get a pencil and paper, I'll tell you how to find us.

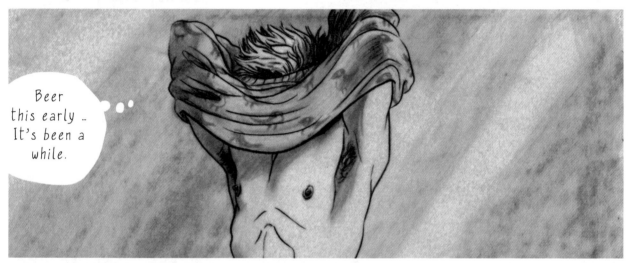

Beer this early ... It's been a while.

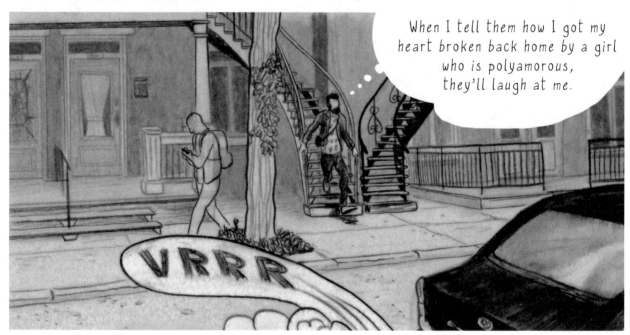

When I tell them how I got my heart broken back home by a girl who is polyamorous, they'll laugh at me.

VRRR

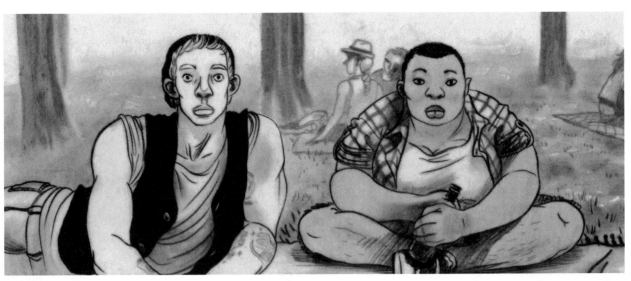

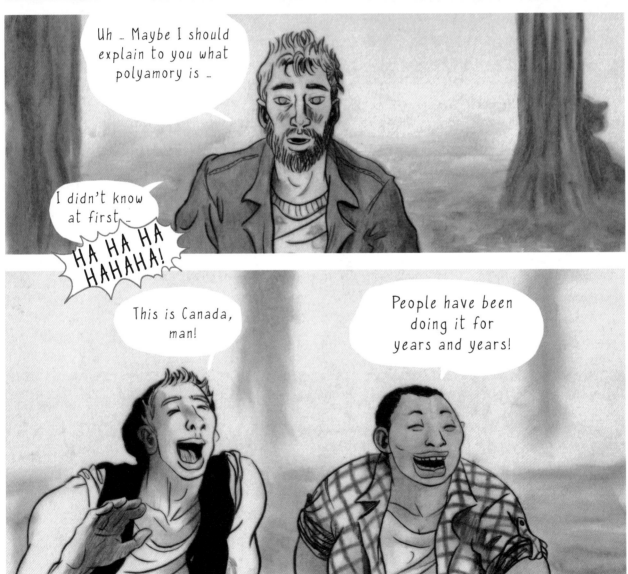

Uh ... Maybe I should explain to you what polyamory is ...

I didn't know at first ...

HA HA HA HAHAHA!

This is Canada, man!

People have been doing it for years and years!

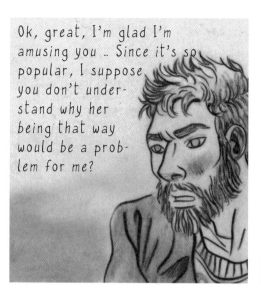

Ok, great, I'm glad I'm amusing you ... Since it's so popular, I suppose you don't understand why her being that way would be a problem for me?

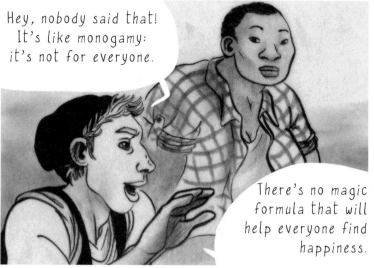

Hey, nobody said that! It's like monogamy: it's not for everyone.

There's no magic formula that will help everyone find happiness.

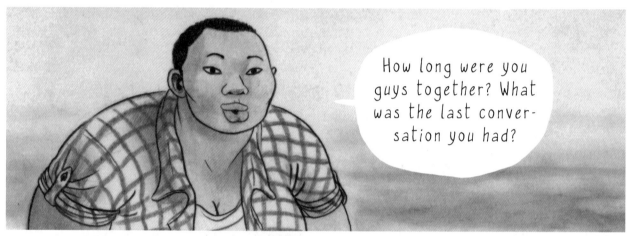

How long were you guys together? What was the last conversation you had?

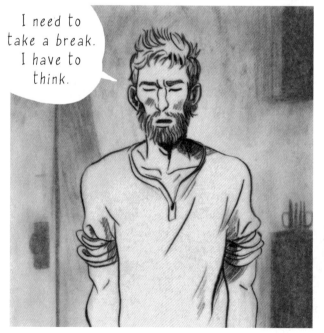

I need to take a break. I have to think.

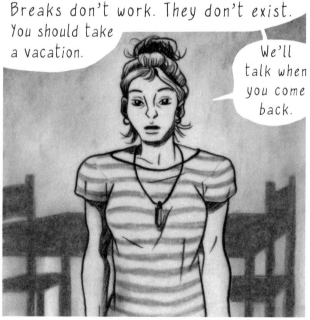

Breaks don't work. They don't exist. You should take a vacation.

We'll talk when you come back.

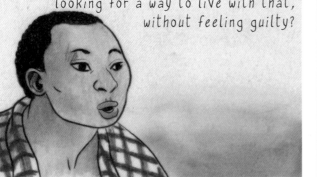

Ok… but what's that mean? What are you afraid of? Why are you freaking out? Because she's got the nerve to tell you she has feelings and desires for several people, including you? And that she's looking for a way to live with that, without feeling guilty?

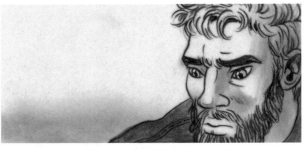

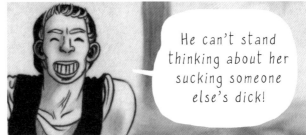

He can't stand thinking about her sucking someone else's dick!

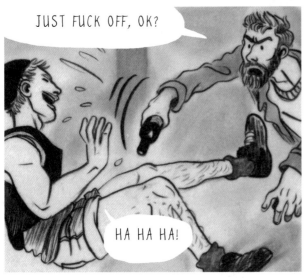

JUST FUCK OFF, OK?

HA HA HA!

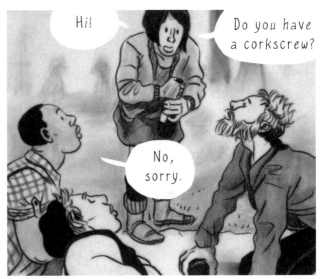

Hi!

Do you have a corkscrew?

No, sorry.

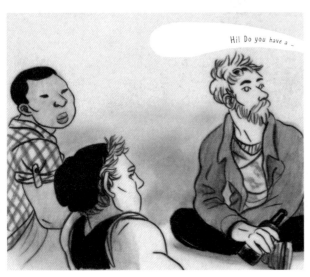

Hi! Do you have a …

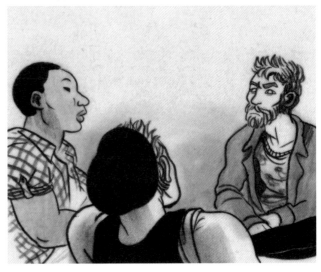

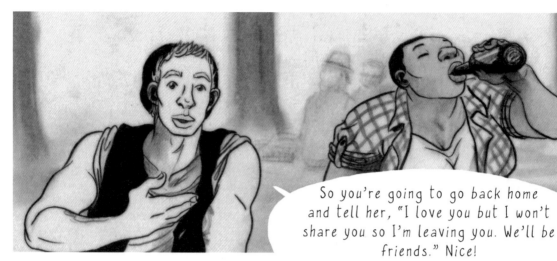

So you're going to go back home and tell her, "I love you but I won't share you so I'm leaving you. We'll be friends." Nice!

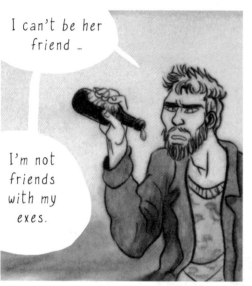

I can't be her friend …

I'm not friends with my exes.

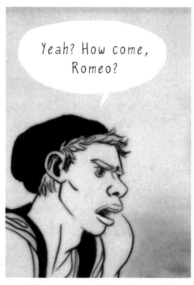

Yeah? How come, Romeo?

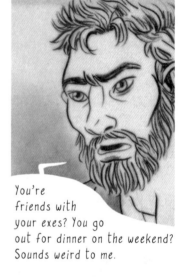

You're friends with your exes? You go out for dinner on the weekend? Sounds weird to me.

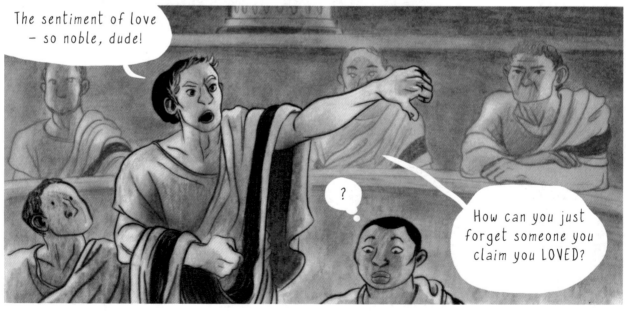

The sentiment of love – so noble, dude!

?

How can you just forget someone you claim you LOVED?

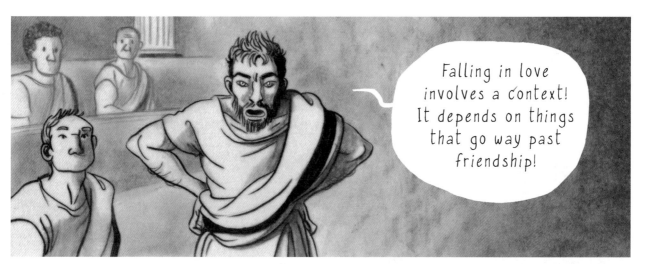

It's not black and white! Some people start out friends and fall in love afterward.

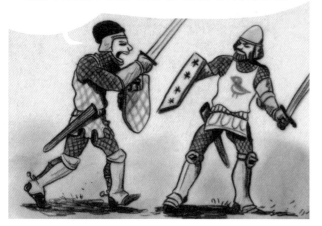

I don't believe in that. There must have been desire from the start!

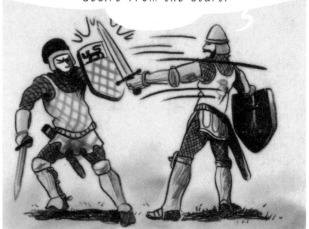

Listen to him, the expert with his package of answers he got at Ikea! He's so sure that luvvv is this sacred, special thing!

I found a corkscrew.

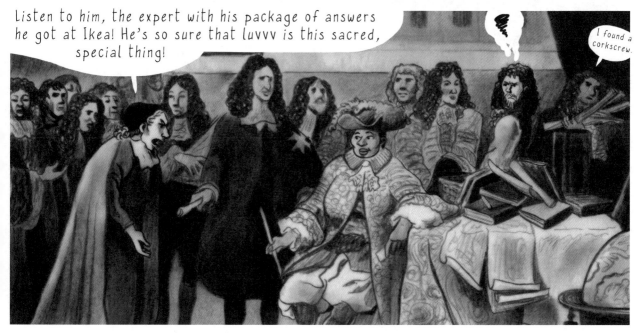

When we met, I felt my life begin ...
Fuck that! That kind of stuff makes me sick!

I think we have to stop making love AND sex into something sacred. Stop making such a big deal about it. Why is it so hard, so risky, so ENORMOUS to tell someone you love them?
When a girl says, "I love you," guys freak out like she told them, "I'm pregnant."
Whatever ... But when there was an intense and intimate connection with someone and a difficult breakup, I can't see myself calling her up and saying, "How's it going? Wanna see a movie? Let's have a drink." That's too bad, but that's how it is!

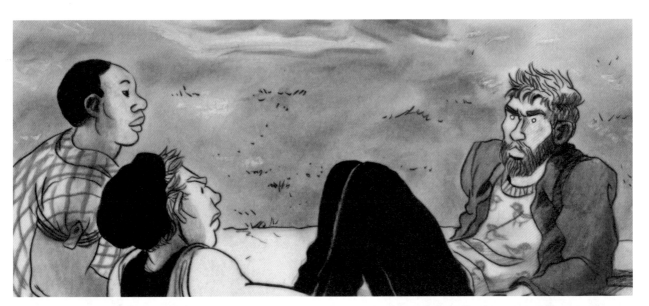

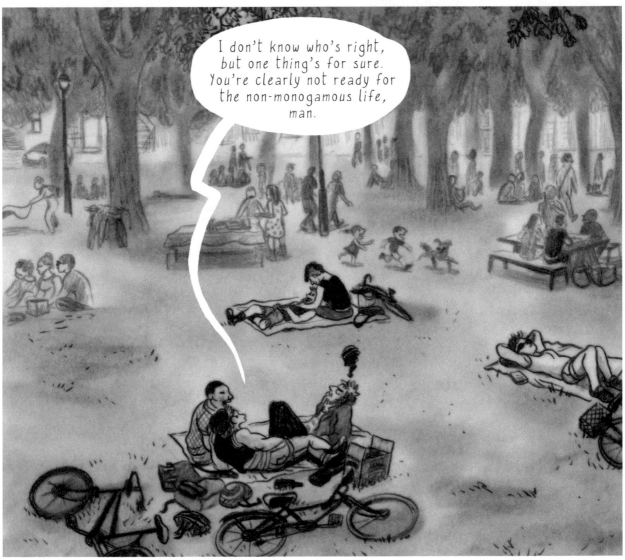

I don't know who's right, but one thing's for sure. You're clearly not ready for the non-monogamous life, man.

8.

Fuck-Buddies

I'd love to make love to you outside, in the summer heat. That would be something we'd always remember.

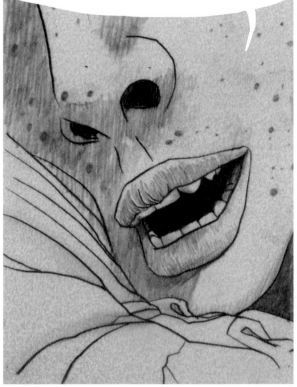

You know I can't risk being seen with you in public. For me it's exciting knowing every Thursday afternoon we'll be together at the hotel.

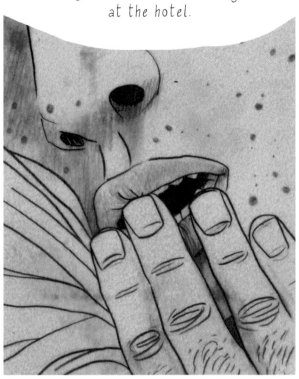

Yeah, but it's been four months now ...

And ...? I thought we were the fuck-buddies of the century. You want to quit?

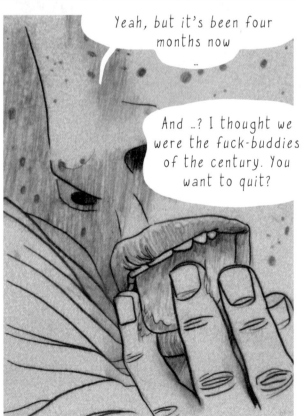

Not at all ... I was just going to ask you: when are you going to tell your wife?

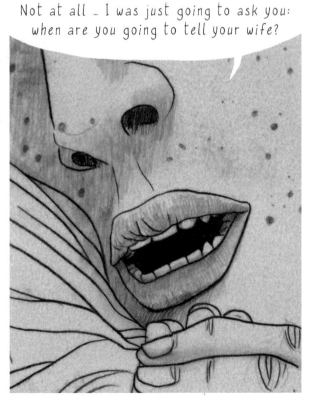

And you, Mr. Morality, don't you have a boyfriend?
Not really. Who are you talking about? Sure, I meet people, but nothing serious since you.

Whatever. You and I are fickle, we're the unfaithful kind. That's why it works with us.
Except that I'm honest with my partners. I'm not hiding behind a straight marriage.

Stop that … If my wife found out, she'd destroy my life and my career too. And she wouldn't think twice about turning my idiot son against me in her divine crusade. No way! The world is full of sharks wearing Dolce & Gabbana. Eat or be eaten — that's the choice.

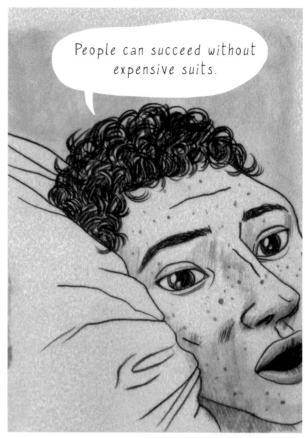

People can succeed without expensive suits.

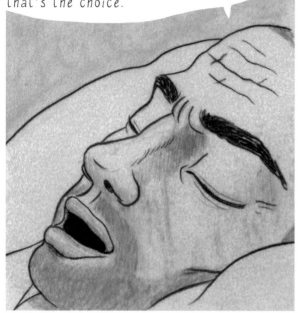

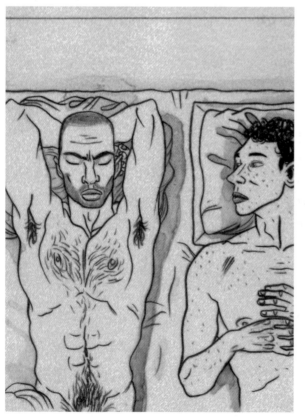

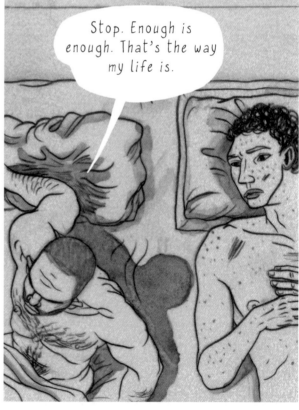

Stop. Enough is enough. That's the way my life is.

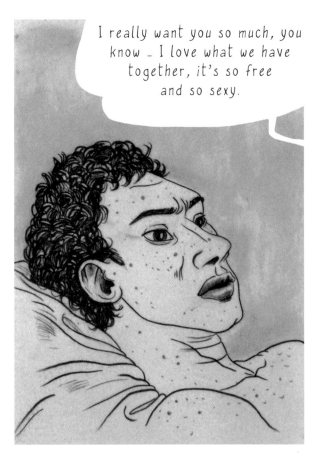

I really want you so much, you know ... I love what we have together, it's so free and so sexy.

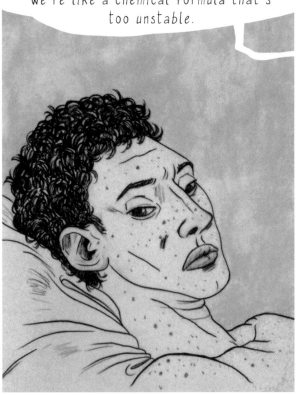

But we can't plan for a future together. We're like a chemical formula that's too unstable.

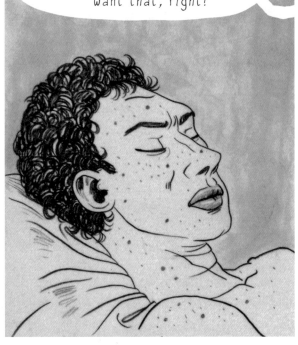

Anyway, planning is just a fantasy, it's not real. What's real is here and now, our Thursdays together. And we both want that, right?

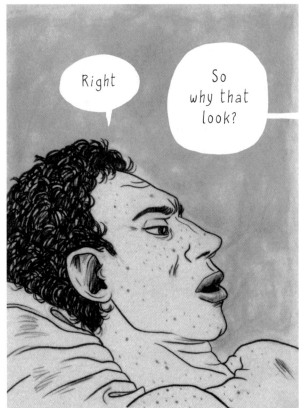

Right

So why that look?

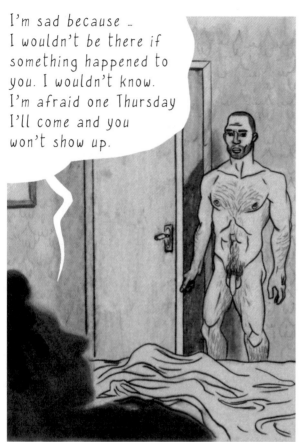

I'm sad because …
I wouldn't be there if
something happened to
you. I wouldn't know.
I'm afraid one Thursday
I'll come and you
won't show up.

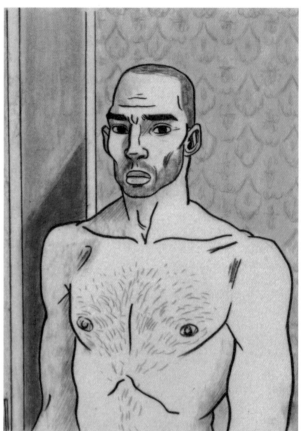

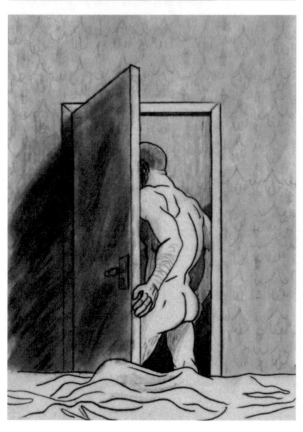

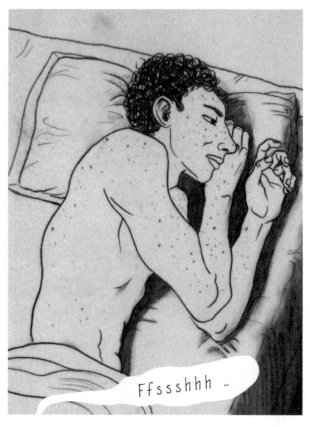

Ffssshhh …

Ffssshhh
Fsh
ffshssshhh

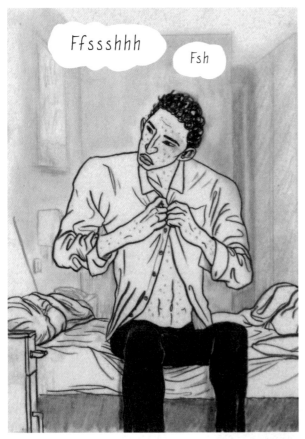

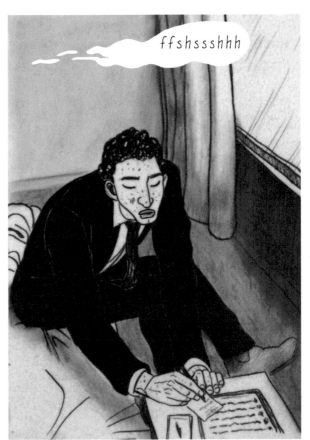

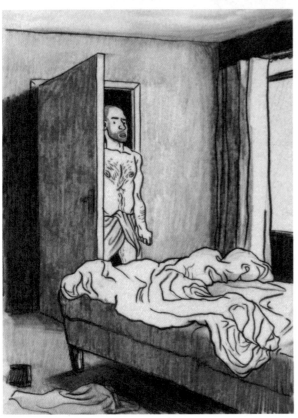

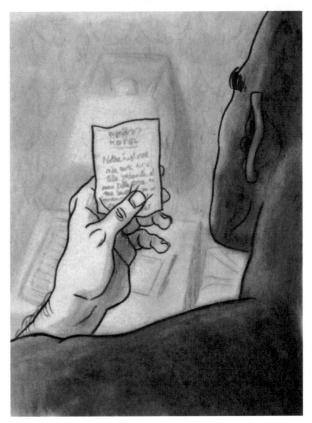

HOTEL
Our affair, that began so suddenly and with such strength, will leave me only a violent memory
Till Thursday

BODOMBODOMBODOMDOMBODOMBODOMBODO

9.

The Confession

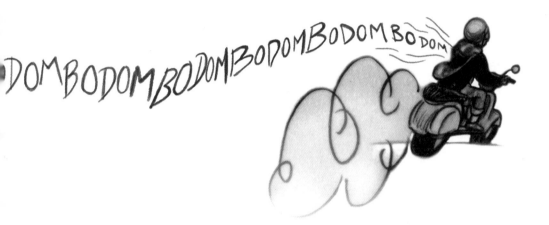

DOMBODOMBODOMBODOMBODOMBODOM

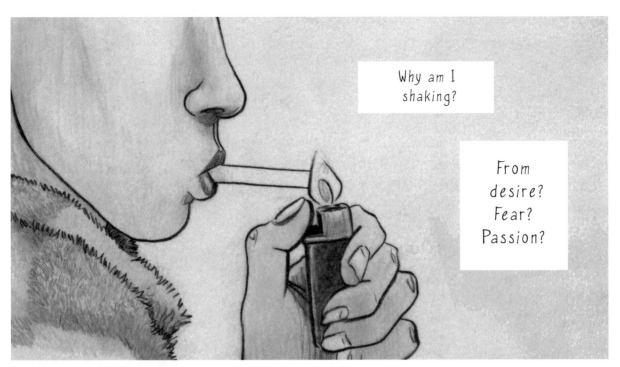

Why am I shaking?

From desire? Fear? Passion?

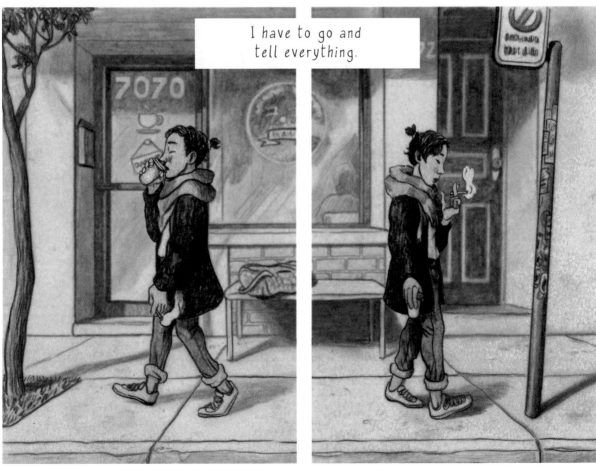

I have to go and tell everything.

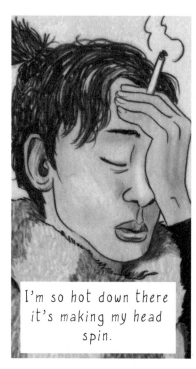

I'm so hot down there it's making my head spin.

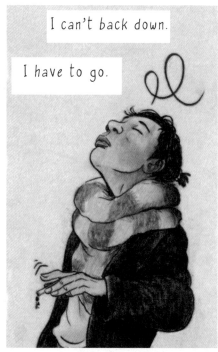

I can't back down.

I have to go.

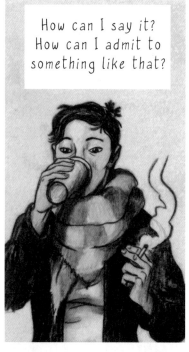

How can I say it? How can I admit to something like that?

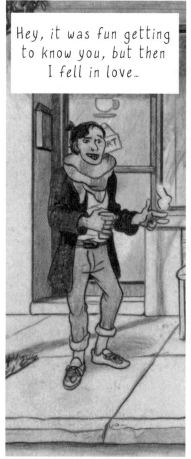

Hey, it was fun getting to know you, but then I fell in love...

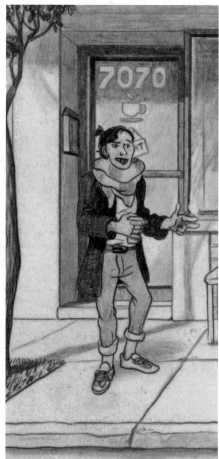

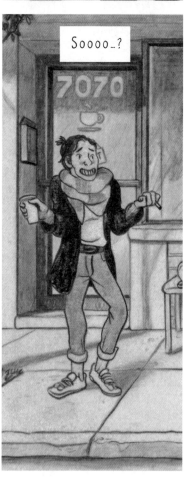

Soooo...?

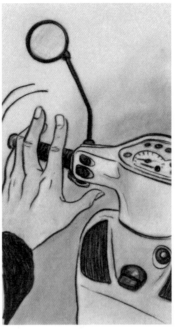

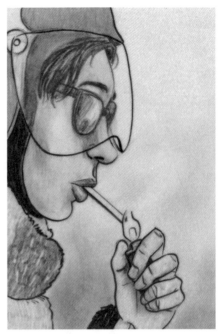

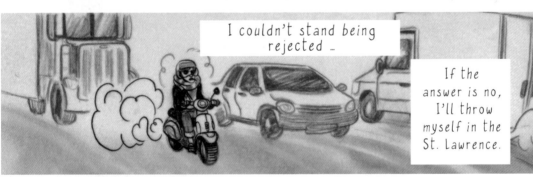

I couldn't stand being rejected ...

If the answer is no, I'll throw myself in the St. Lawrence.

Or go to the Gaspé and punch a bear in the nose.

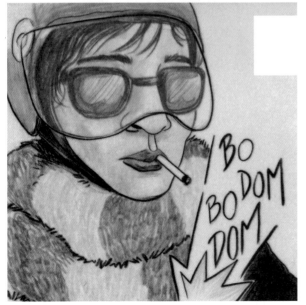

BO BO DOM DOM

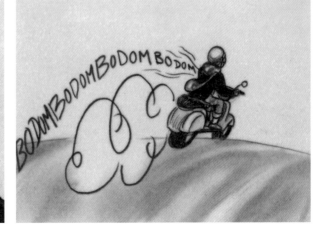

BODOMBODOMBODOMBODOM

RIIING
BOM

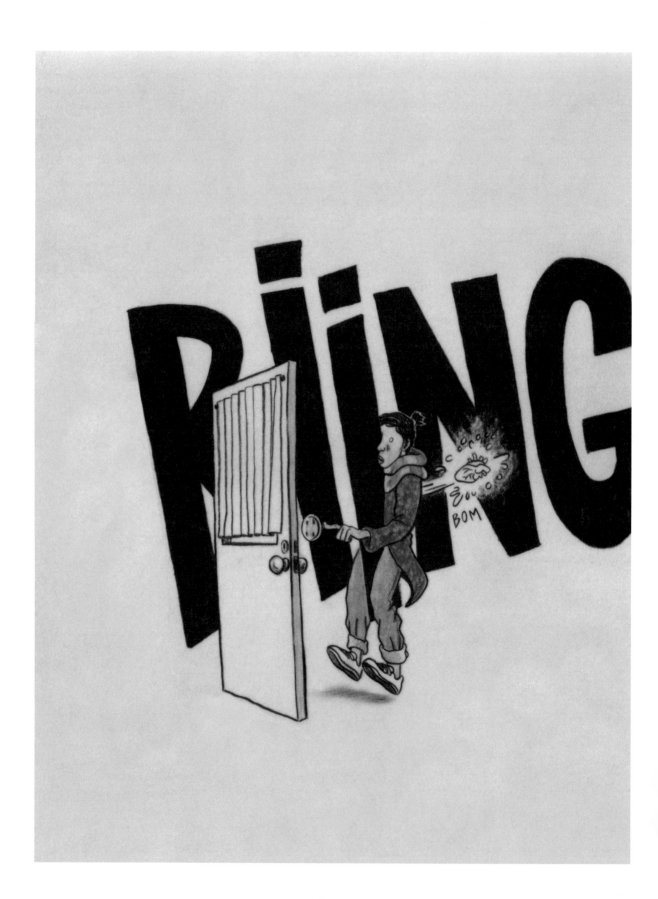

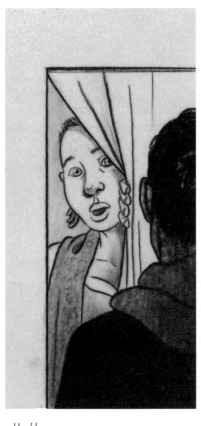

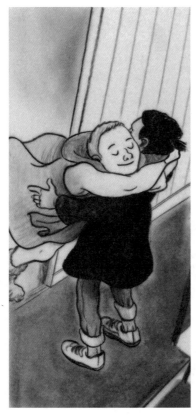

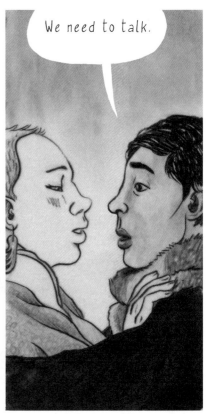
We need to talk.

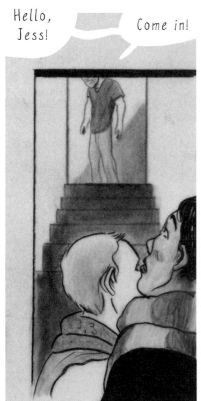
Hello, Jess!
Come in!

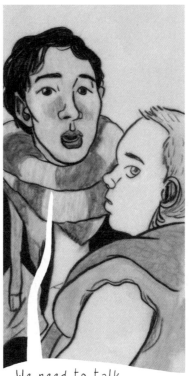
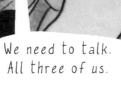
We need to talk.
All three of us.

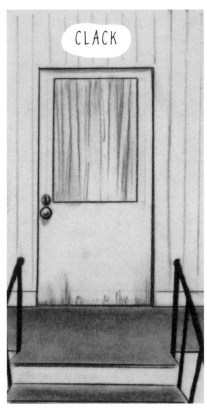
CLACK

Coffee, Jess?
No thanks, I've had my fill.
BODOM BODOM BODOM
You know, being with you has been so good for me, you've given me new life.
The way we met, the first night the three of us slept together, the intensity, the intimacy we created ...
I think you feel the same thing– there's an understanding between us three.

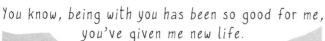

I would have never thought something like this would happen to me. But now I can't imagine living any other way.
Listen ...
If I don't tell you, I'll die ...
I want to be with you ... I want us to share this love together. Us three. I'm ready for it. For you.
I feel it every time I look at you, the air is buzzing with it. I don't just want a night's pleasure once in a while.
I want to wake up with you two in the morning, I want us to cook together and have projects together, and do the things we like together and always be united in hard times.

It's so good *being with you*, it makes me so proud. It's so beautiful and light, what I feel, that I want to shout it from the rooftops, all day and all night.

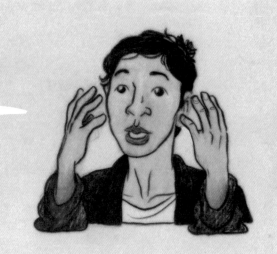

Hell, my love for you is a revolt against this shitty world!

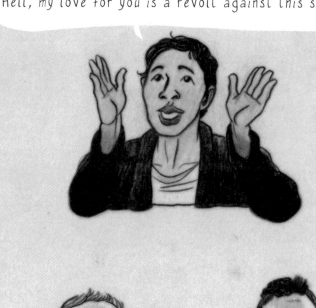

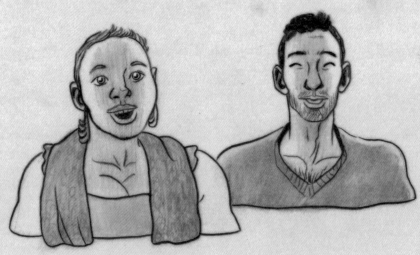

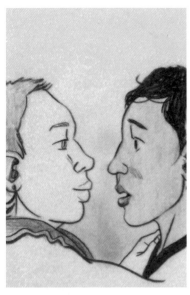
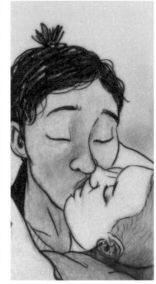
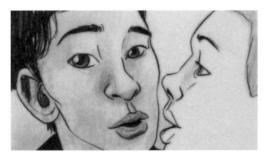
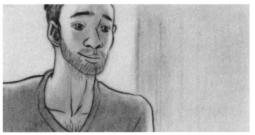

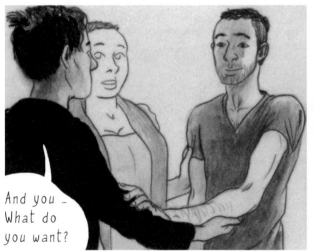

And you ...
What do
you want?

We were hoping you'd bring it up first!

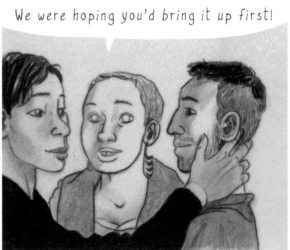

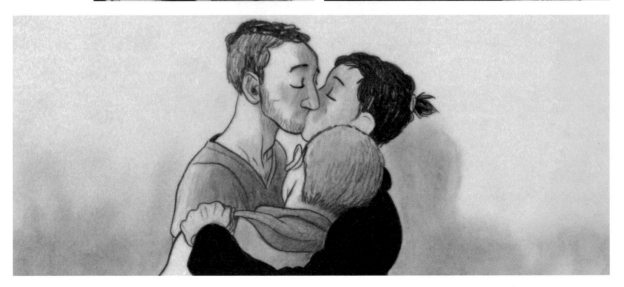

My heart's going
to explode.

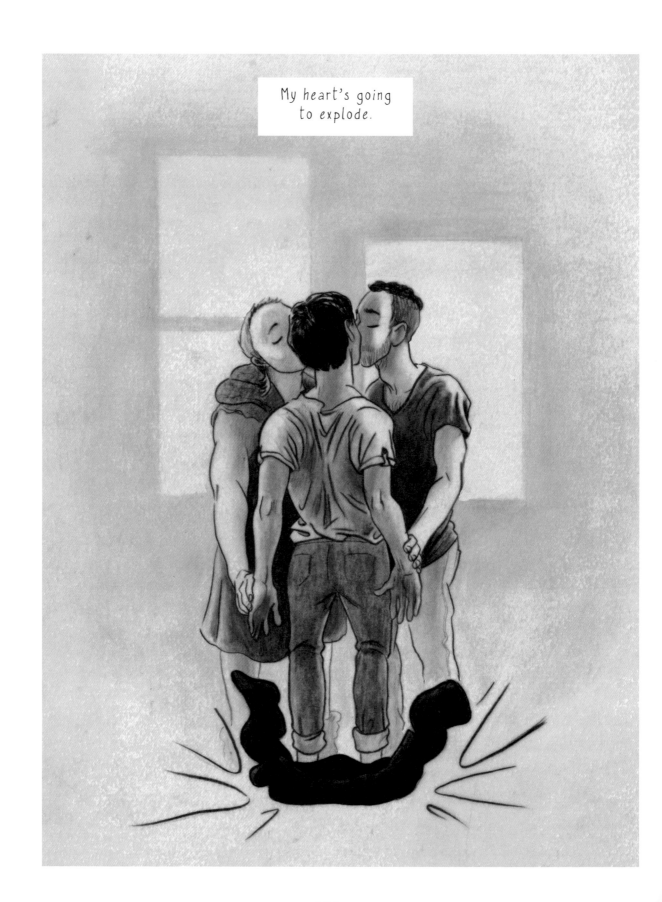

10.

After the Fight

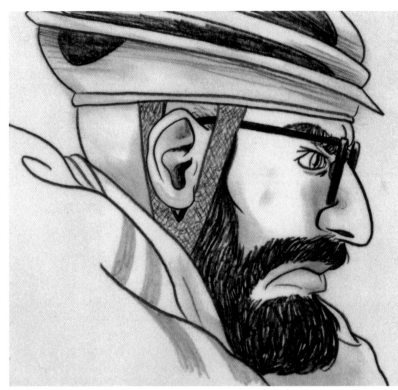

Feeling your life break right in two. Another endless fight, one retort too many. My vocal cords stretched so tight they're about to snap.

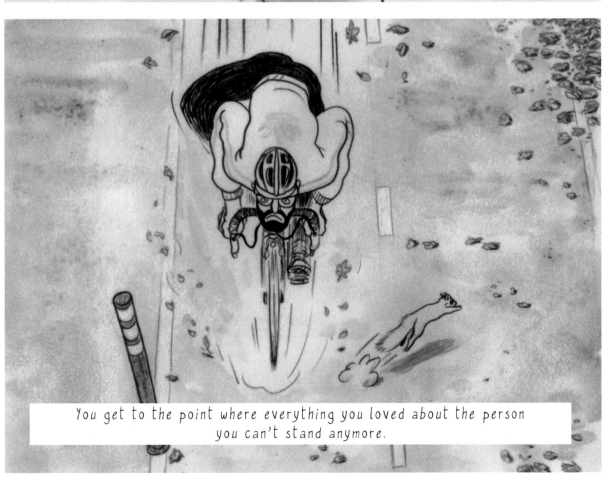

You get to the point where everything you loved about the person you can't stand anymore.

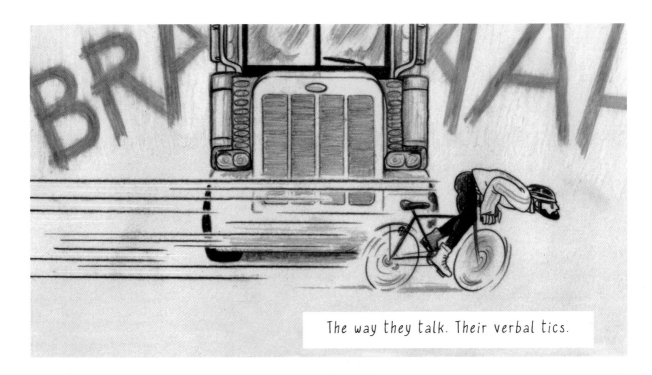

The way they talk. Their verbal tics.

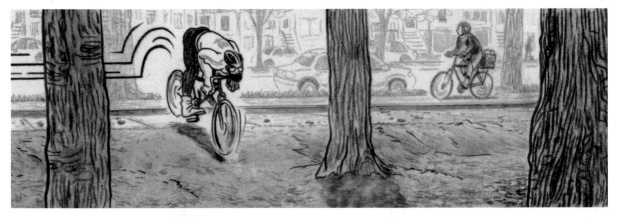

The way they
fix their hair.
Their voice …
yelling what
you don't
want to hear.

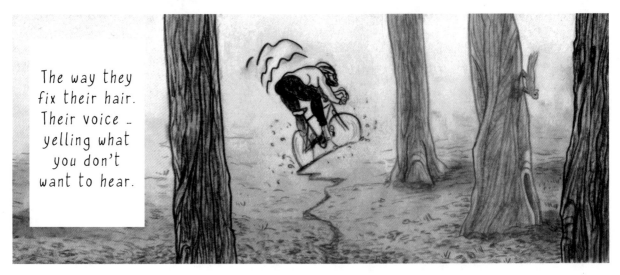

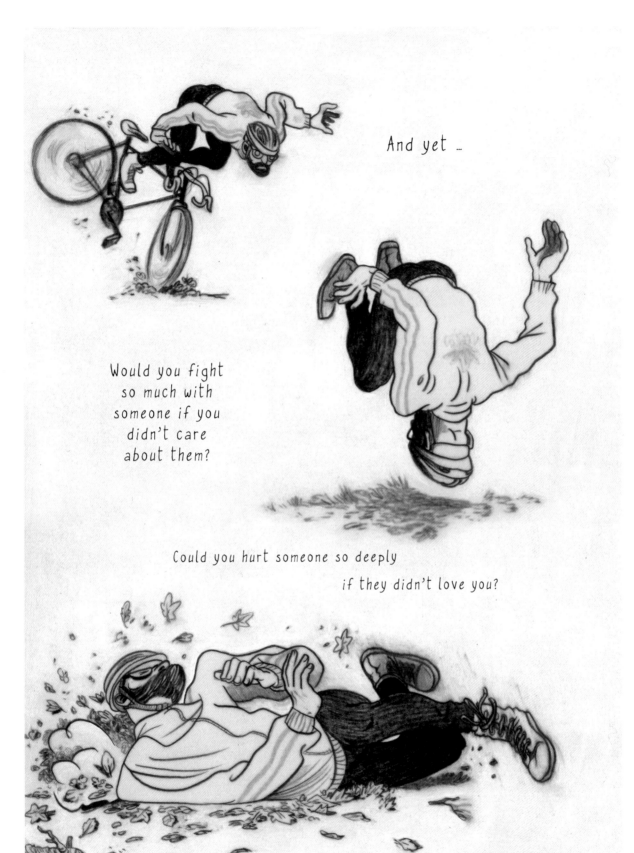

And yet ...

Would you fight
so much with
someone if you
didn't care
about them?

Could you hurt someone so deeply

if they didn't love you?

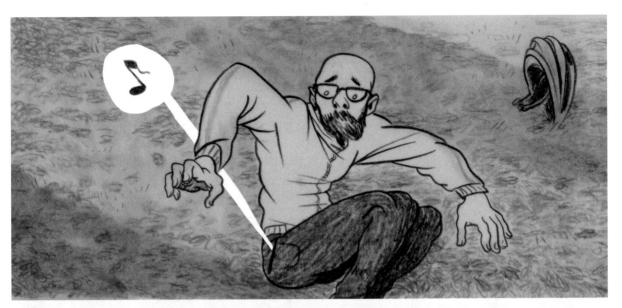

The whole language between us has changed, it makes my blood run cold. Everything that was part of what we shared has pushed me to the very edge.

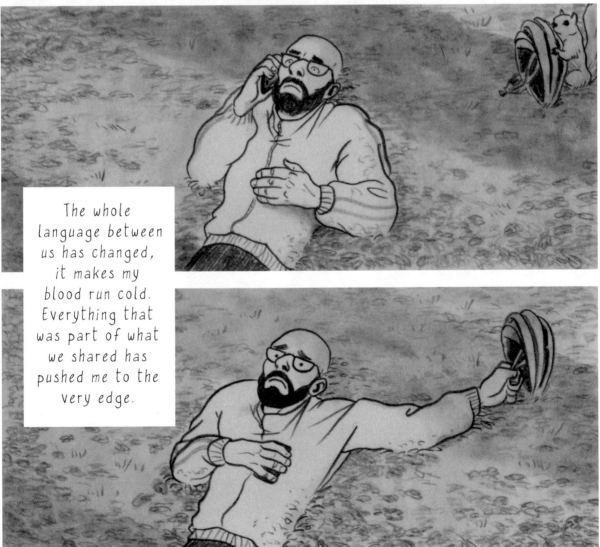

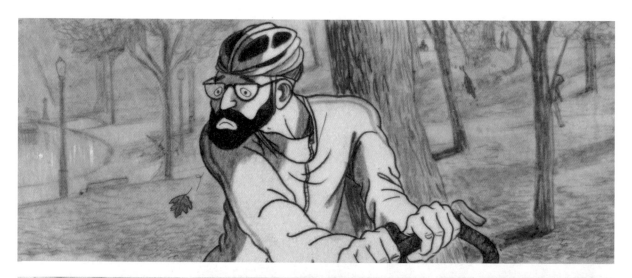

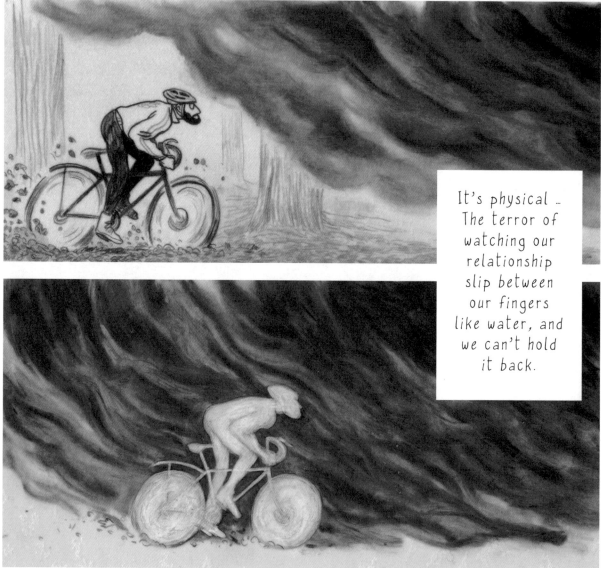

It's physical ...
The terror of
watching our
relationship
slip between
our fingers
like water, and
we can't hold
it back.

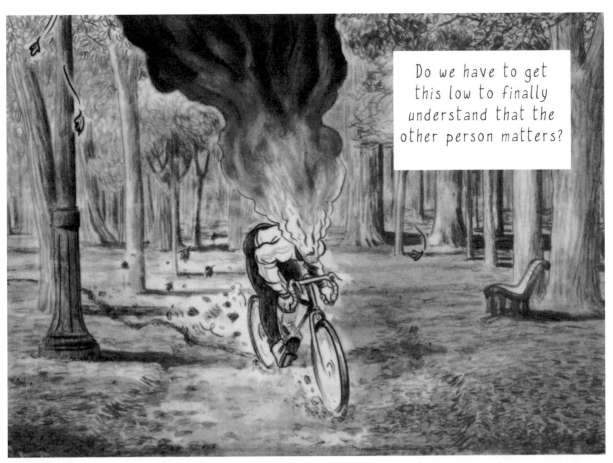

Do we have to get this low to finally understand that the other person matters?

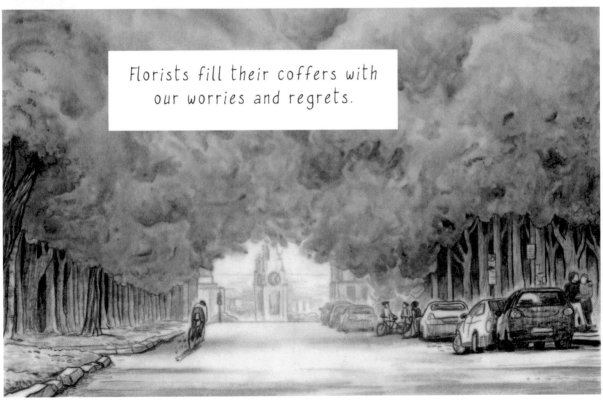

Florists fill their coffers with our worries and regrets.

11.

The Cute Girl
Next Door

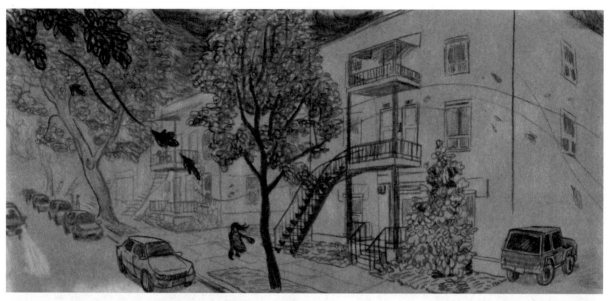

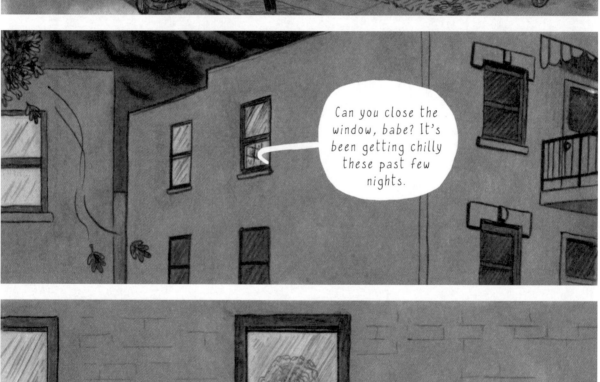

Can you close the window, babe? It's been getting chilly these past few nights.

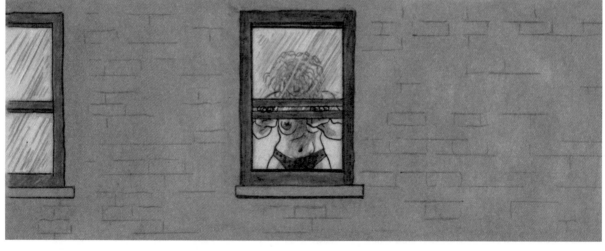

Now ...
Where
were
we at,
you and me?

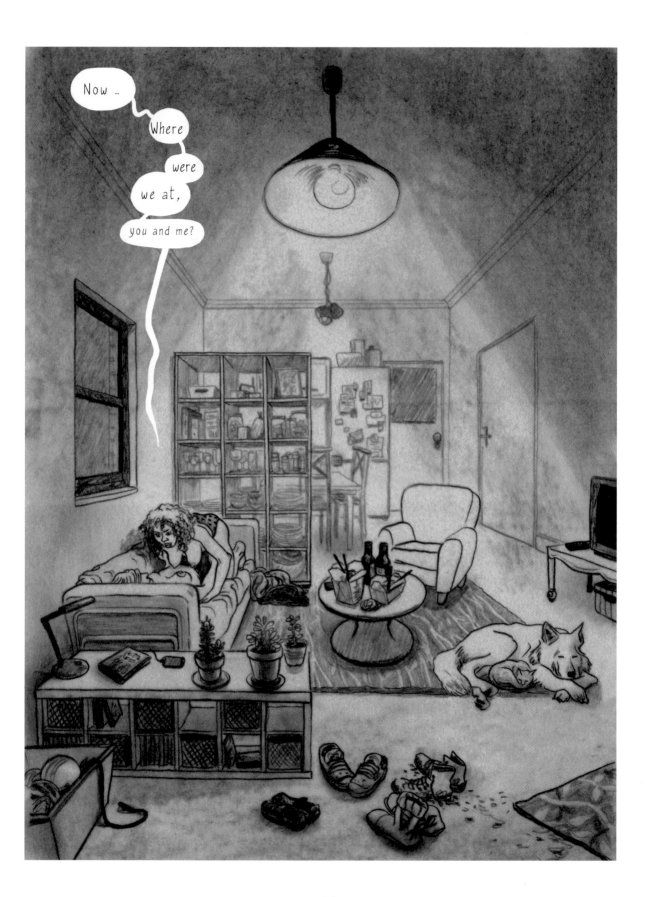

RING
RRING!
RRRIING!
Who cares? Just don't stop.

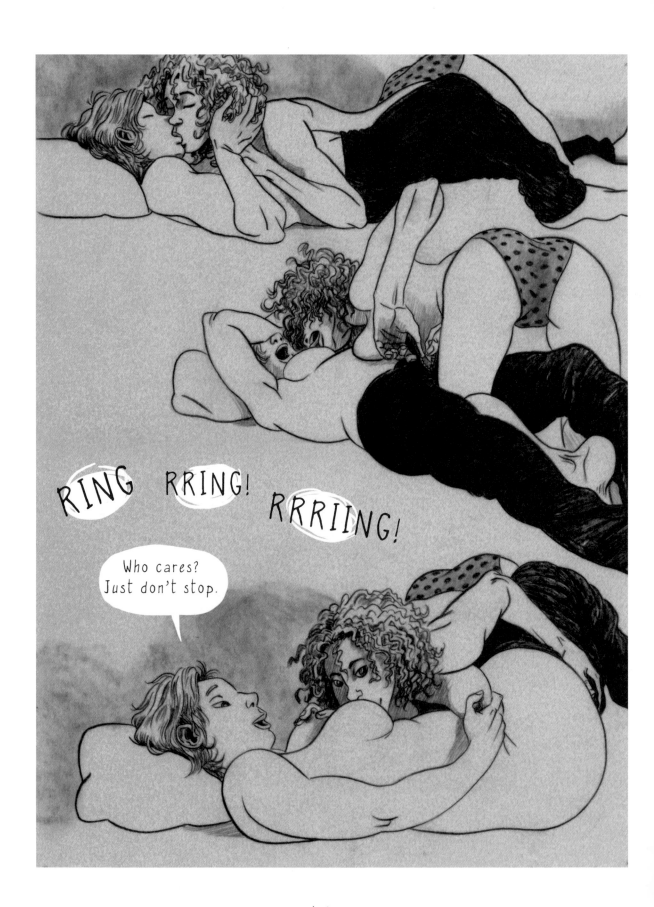

RING!
I won't! Besides, I'm sure it's your mother. She has a way of calling at the worst time.
aaaah
?
AAAAH

...!
aaa
aa
hhh
AAH !
ah
Ah-ha! The cute girl next door got herself a new guy!
AAH!
AH!
AAAAAAH!

Hell … Come here, stud-man, and kiss me!
BAILLE
Ha ha … Mmm. <smack smack> I love you, you know.

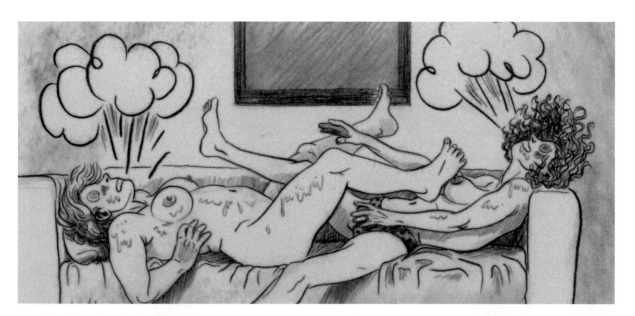

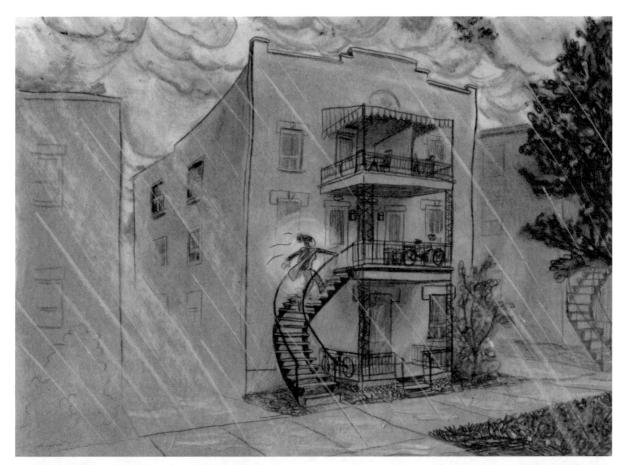

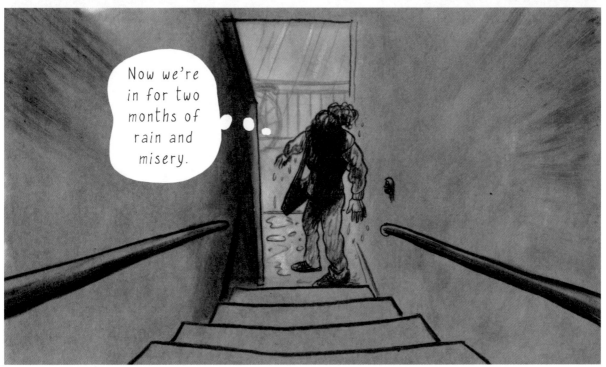

Now we're in for two months of rain and misery.

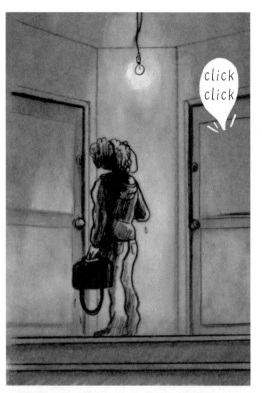

click
click

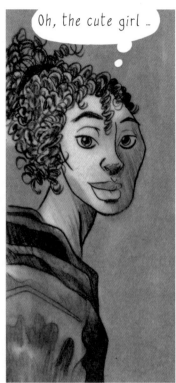

Oh, the cute girl ...

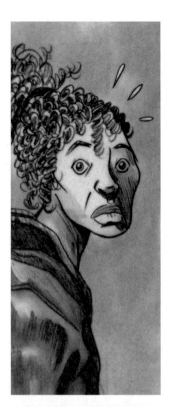

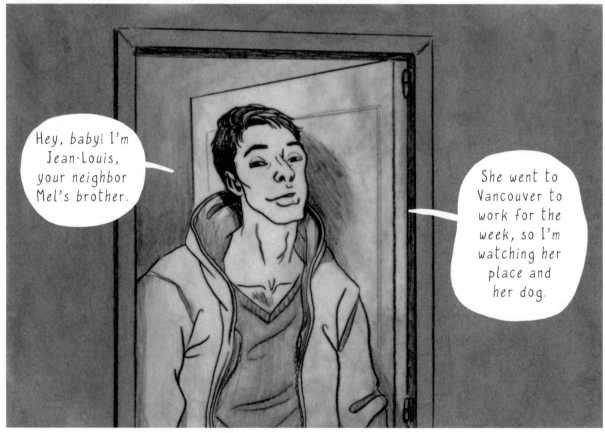

Hey, baby! I'm Jean-Louis, your neighbor Mel's brother.

She went to Vancouver to work for the week, so I'm watching her place and her dog.

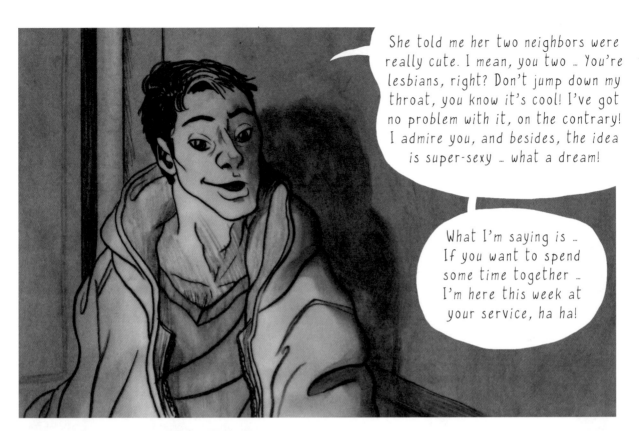

She told me her two neighbors were really cute. I mean, you two ... You're lesbians, right? Don't jump down my throat, you know it's cool! I've got no problem with it, on the contrary! I admire you, and besides, the idea is super-sexy ... what a dream!

What I'm saying is ... If you want to spend some time together ... I'm here this week at your service, ha ha!

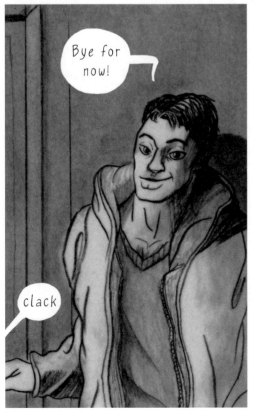

Bye for now!

clack

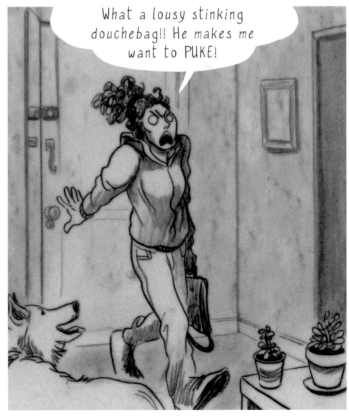

What a lousy stinking douchebag!! He makes me want to PUKE!

Hey … The cute girl next door found herself a new guy. Don't you think that's exciting?
aa aaa ah!
N-O spells No.

12.

Back at Dawn

CHIPS
CHIPS

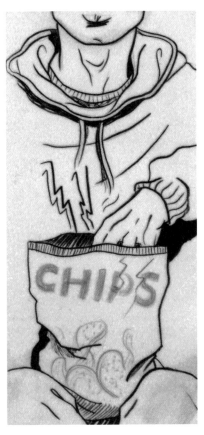

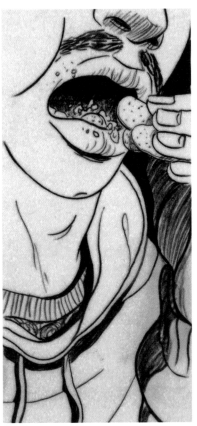

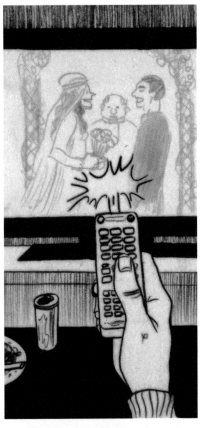

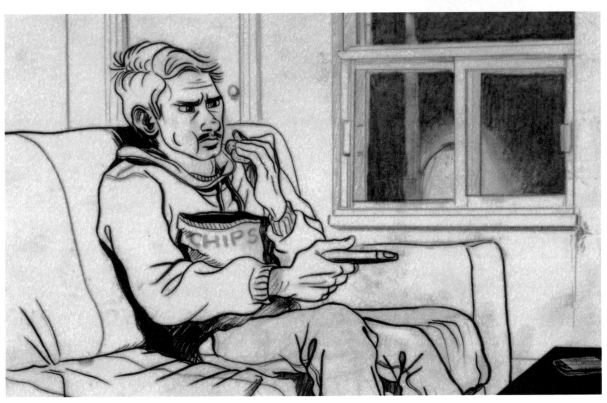

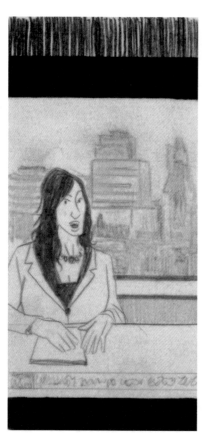

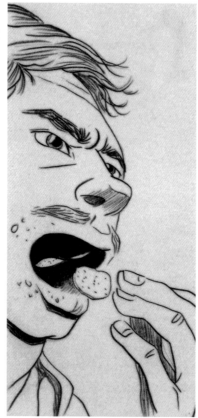

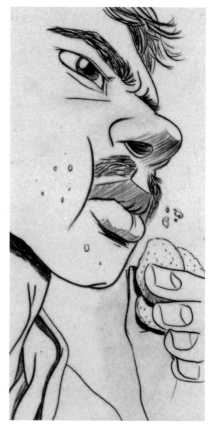

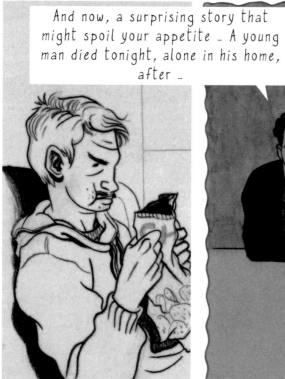

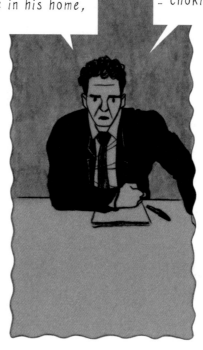

And now, a surprising story that might spoil your appetite … A young man died tonight, alone in his home, after …

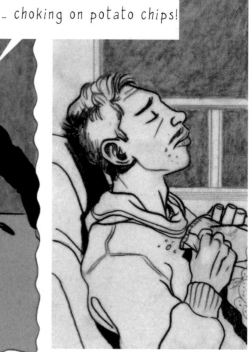

… choking on potato chips!

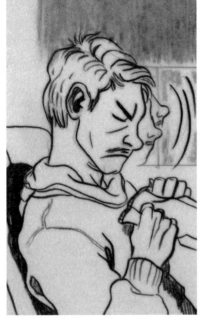

According to investigators, he was extremely upset that his partner could not be reached on his cell phone.

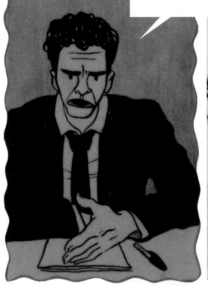

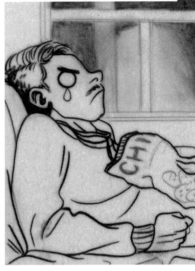

It should be noted that his partner had gone out to dinner with HIS EX! To disappear like that into the night — suspicious indeed! Any one of us would choke on potato chips too *if* it happened to us!

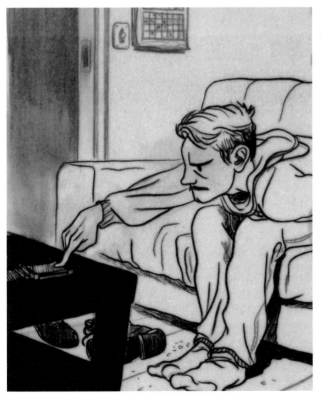

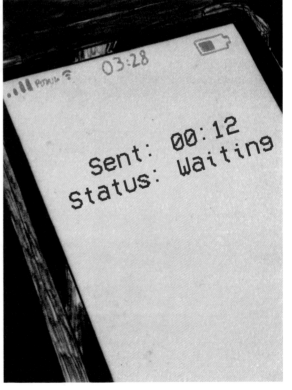

Sent: 00:12
Status: Waiting

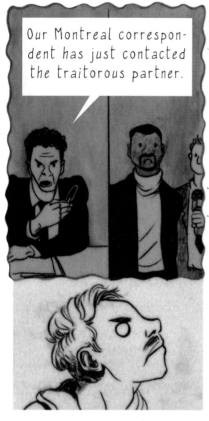

Our Montreal correspondent has just contacted the traitorous partner.

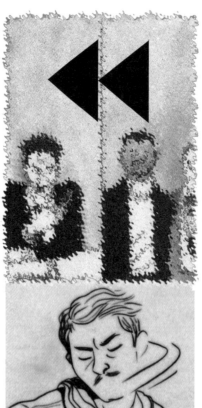

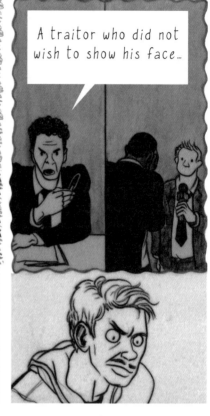

A traitor who did not wish to show his face...

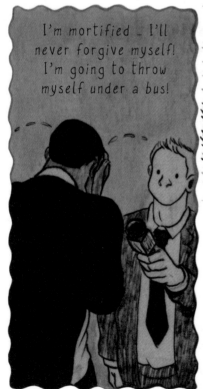

I'm mortified ... I'll never forgive myself! I'm going to throw myself under a bus!

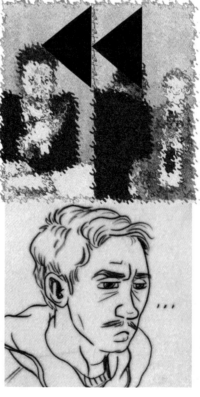

...

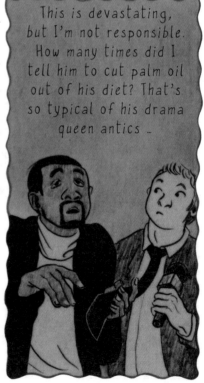

This is devastating, but I'm not responsible. How many times did I tell him to cut palm oil out of his diet? That's so typical of his drama queen antics ...

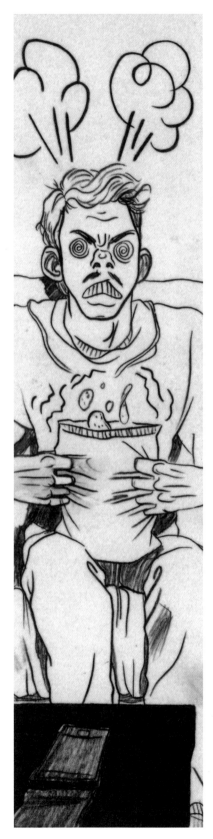

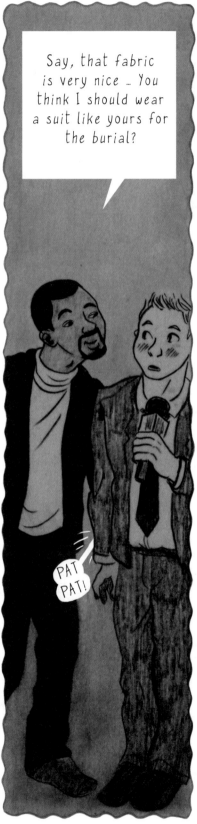

Say, that fabric is very nice ... You think I should wear a suit like yours for the burial?

PAT PAT!

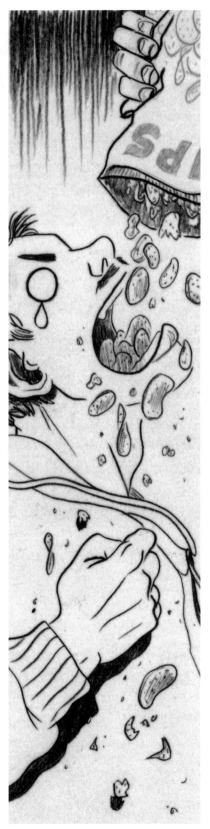

157

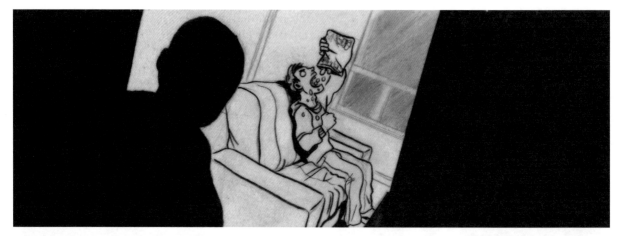

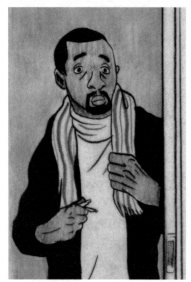

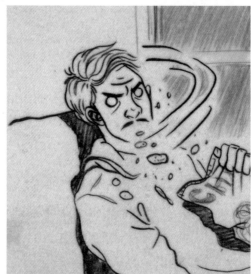

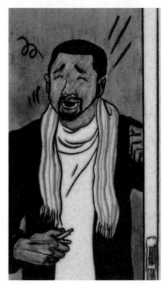

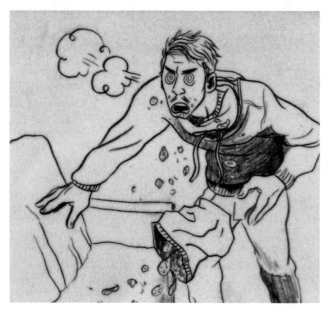

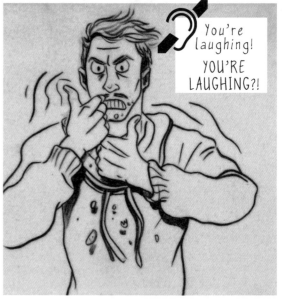

You're laughing! YOU'RE LAUGHING?!

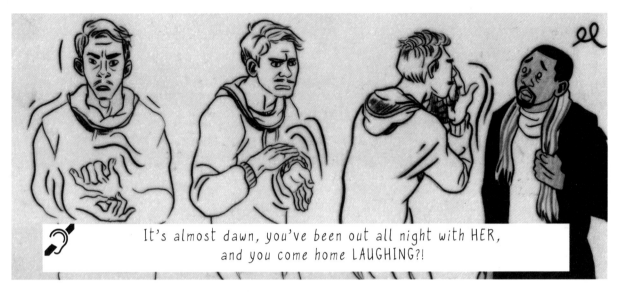

It's almost dawn, you've been out all night with HER, and you come home LAUGHING?!

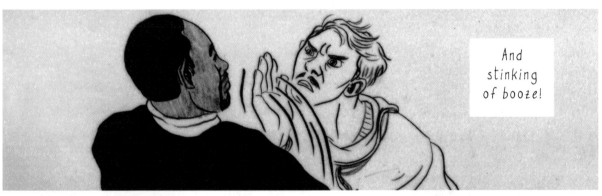

And stinking of booze!

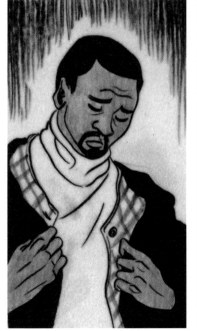

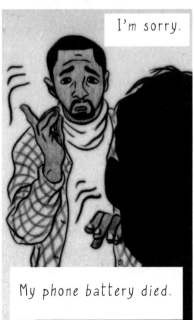

I'm sorry.

My phone battery died.

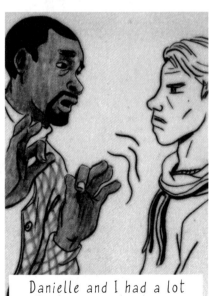

Danielle and I had a lot to talk about, it was important.

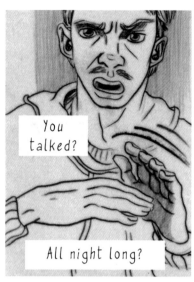

You
talked?

All night long?

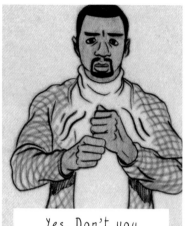

Yes. Don't you
trust me?

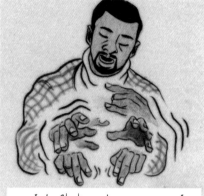

I left two hours ago. I
walked but I'd drunk too
much ... I got lost.

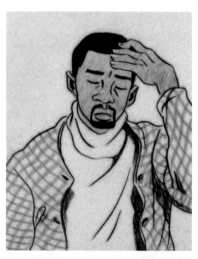

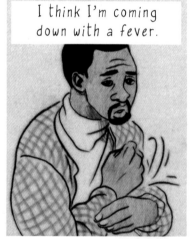

I think I'm coming
down with a fever.

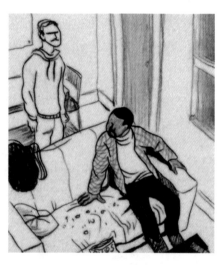

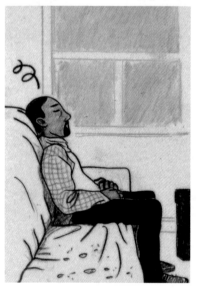

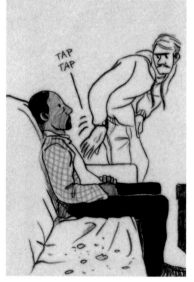

TAP
TAP

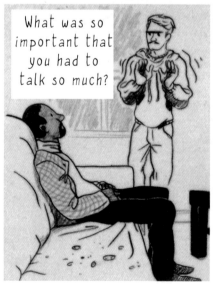

What was so
important that
you had to
talk so much?

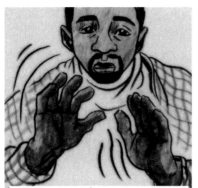

Things about our break-up that she doesn't accept. She misses our relationship, she wanted to know where I was at in my life ...

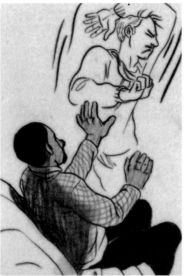

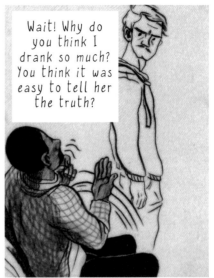

Wait! Why do you think I drank so much? You think it was easy to tell her the truth?

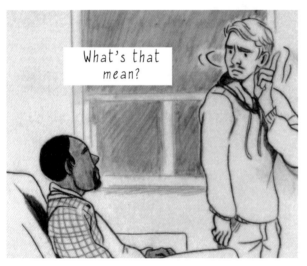

What's that mean?

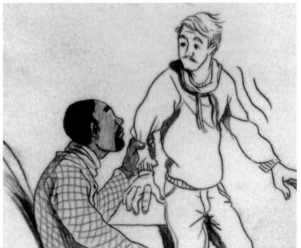

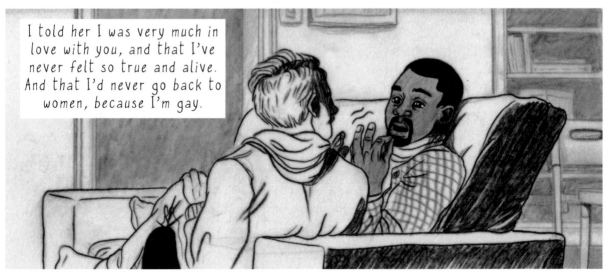

I told her I was very much in love with you, and that I've never felt so true and alive. And that I'd never go back to women, because I'm gay.

161

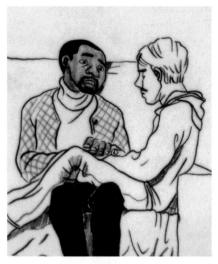

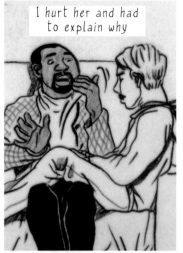

I hurt her and had
to explain why

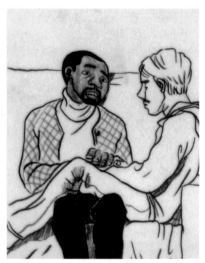

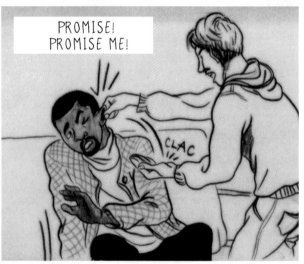

PROMISE!
PROMISE ME!

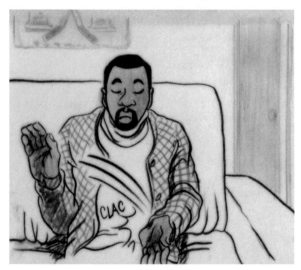

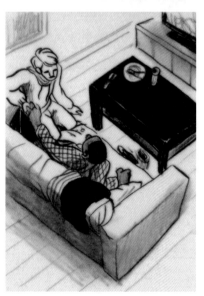

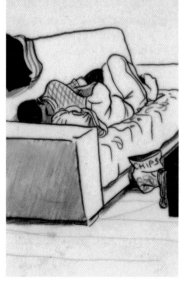

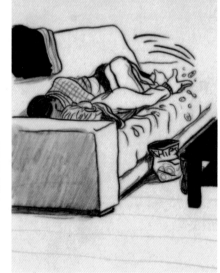

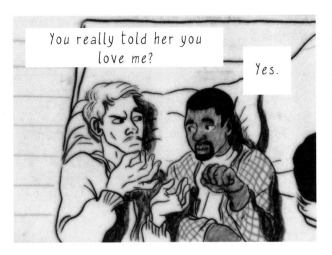

You really told her you love me?

Yes.

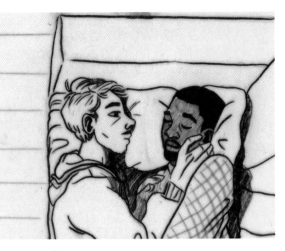

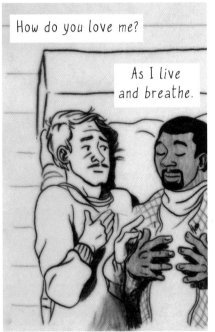

How do you love me?

As I live and breathe.

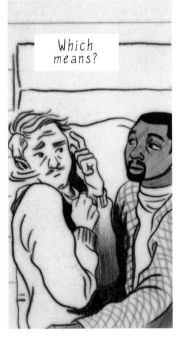

Which means?

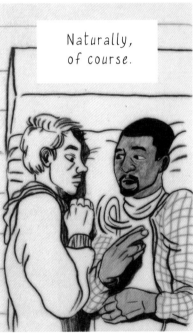

Naturally, of course.

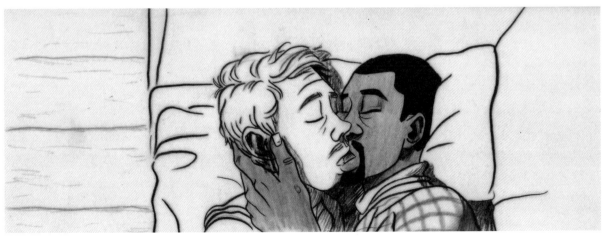

I'd throw myself under a bus if anything happened to you.
Let's talk about living, not dying, okay? You're a worse drama queen than me.

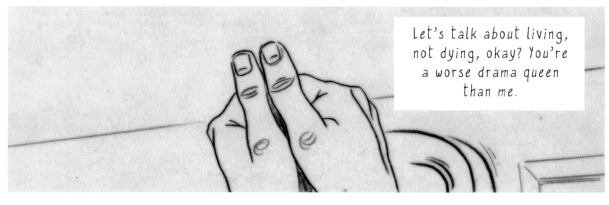

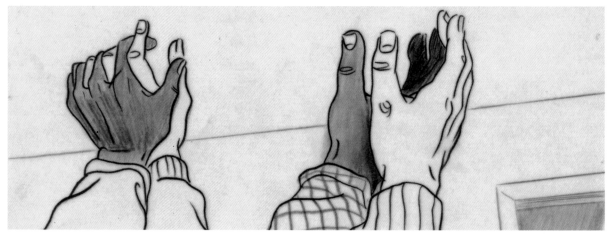

13.

The Break,
the Wait

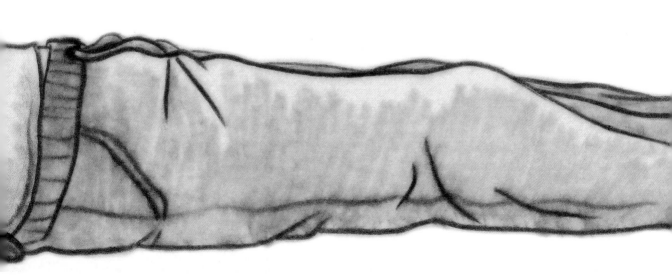

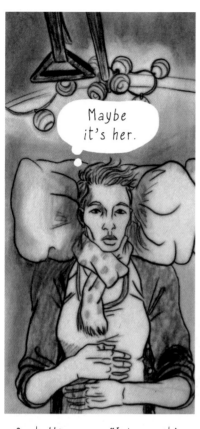

Maybe it's her.

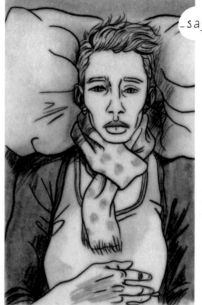

Okay, we said we wouldn't write for a week, we wouldn't talk ... But maybe it's her anyway ...

...saying...

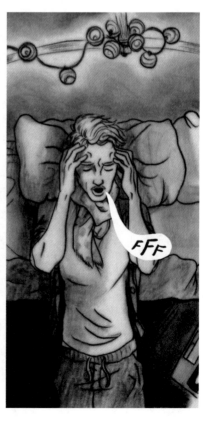

... telling me she's thought it over, she knows it's really over and I should come get my things.

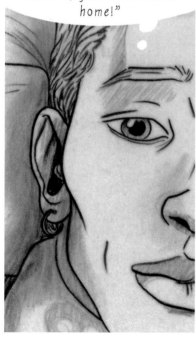

Or telling me, "I know it's only *been* two days, babe, but I miss you too much, fuck it, just come back home!"

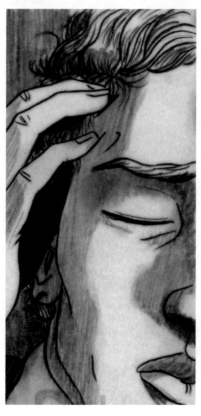

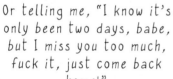

FFF

173

Or maybe … that's what she's waiting for? Maybe she's hoping for that leap, a great declaration?

Fuck … I'm so afraid nothing I do will bring her back … It's burning a hole in me.

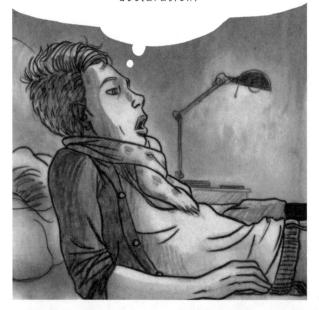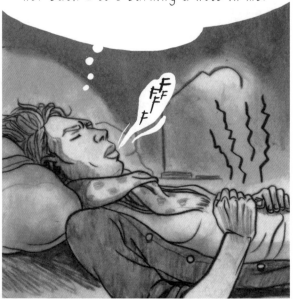

If I went to see her … But how can I just show up if we're taking a break? "It's me?" The idea that you have a place in someone's life … "It's me," and it can't be anyone else knocking at your door, no one else you'd be waiting for, no one else who would say those words.

"It's me" knocking, standing outside your door … The more I think about it, the more I feel the real meaning of those simple words, and how they could play against me. What kind of attitude might win her over? Asserting what I am in her life, or not saying the words because she wants to live without definitions?

AAAH! DYKES!
Hello, psychological suicide!

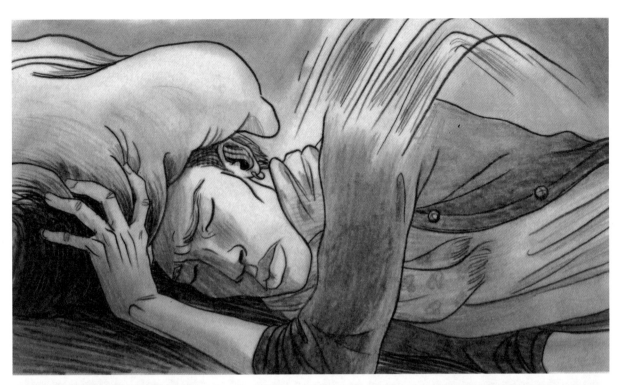

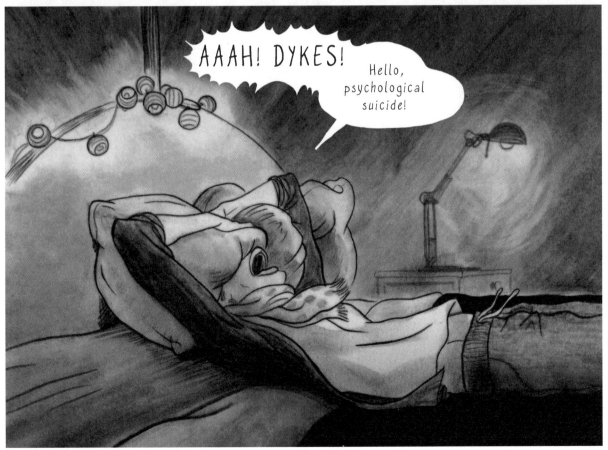

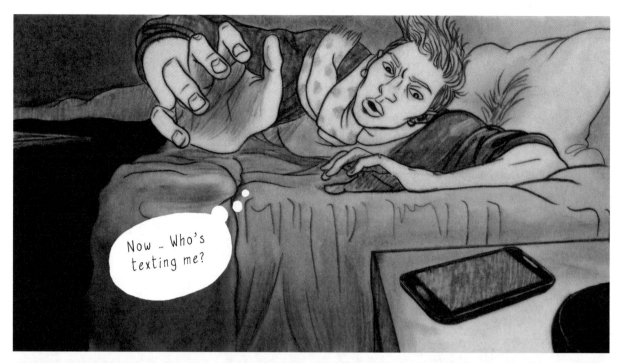

Now … Who's texting me?

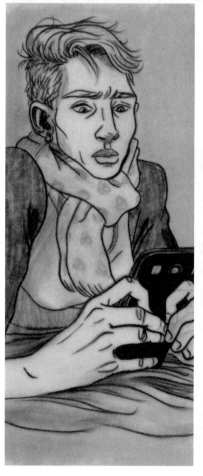

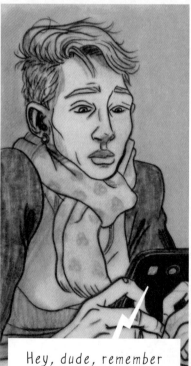

Hey, dude, remember that Owen Pallett is in concert tonight? Hustle your buns, I'll wait for you at the subway!

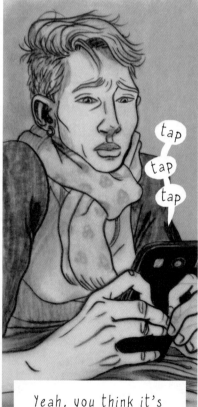

tap

tap

tap

Yeah, you think it's wheelchair accessible?

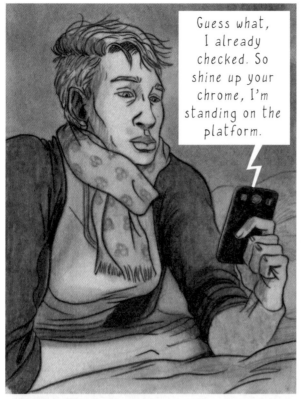

Guess what, I already checked. So shine up your chrome, I'm standing on the platform.

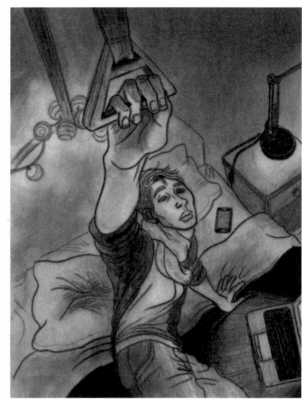

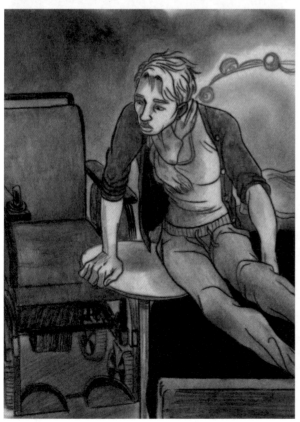

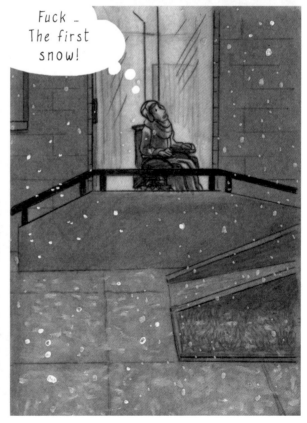

Fuck ...
The first snow!

That message can wait.

14.

The Ghost of Illness

I'm hungry...
I'm coming, sweetie. Go tell your sister that dinner's on in fifteen minutes.

No, it happens all the time, it's our pattern. At least I think so ...

Our fights used to have positive results. You know, when you jump into bed afterward and make love like crazy ...

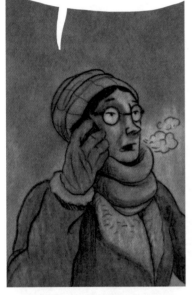

But now our fights just leave us exhausted, because physically, you know, I'm not up to it.

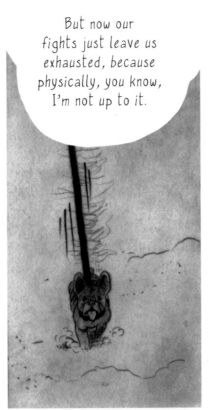

Maybe we're just repeating the pattern and hoping for a final reconciliation.

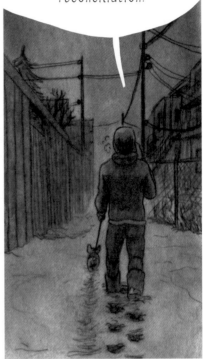

Isn't that what neurosis is? Repeating the same thing and expecting different results?

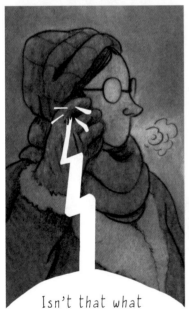

Hey, Dr. Freud! I didn't ask you!

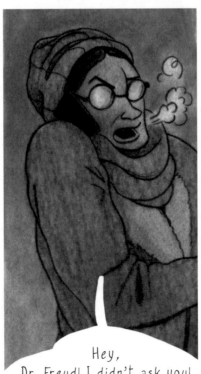

You're the one who called me, honey!

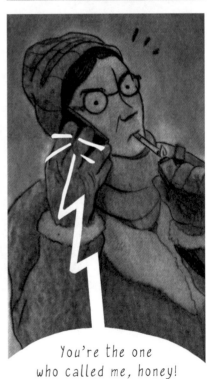

How much do I owe you? What's your hourly rate?
Are you smoking? You know you shouldn't in your condition.
The hell with ...
What? Holy shit!

DISGUSTING!
How come you shit as much as a triceratops? You looking for trouble too?

Where does infidelity begin?

And boredom?
SNAP

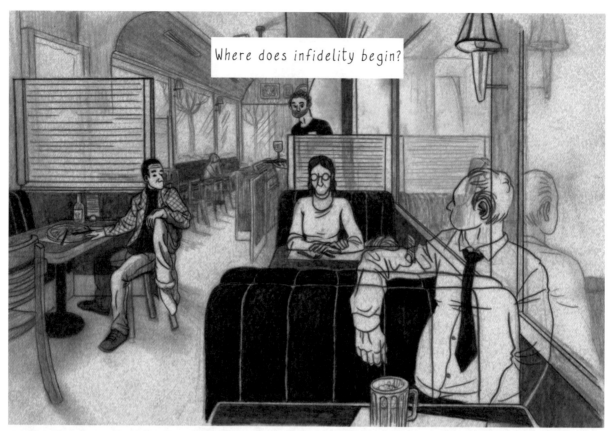

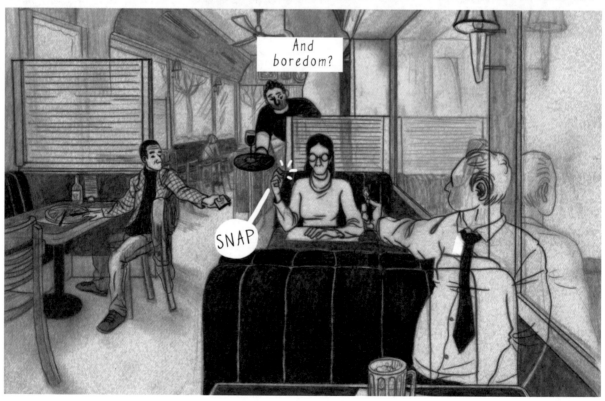

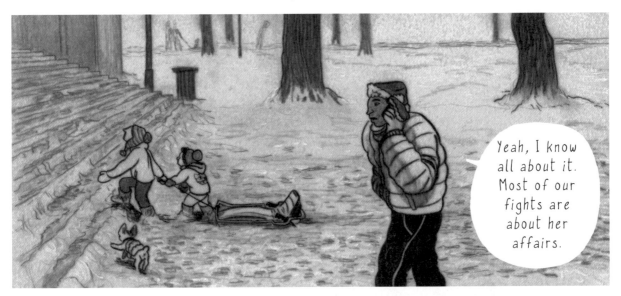

Yeah, I know all about it. Most of our fights are about her affairs.

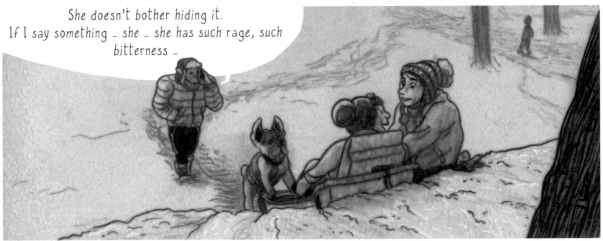

She doesn't bother hiding it. If I say something ... she ... she has such rage, such bitterness ...

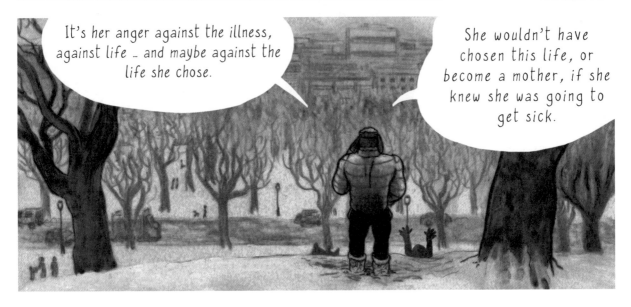

It's her anger against the illness, against life ... and maybe against the life she chose.

She wouldn't have chosen this life, or become a mother, if she knew she was going to get sick.

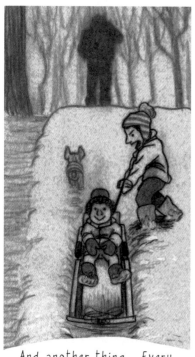

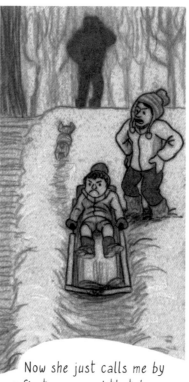

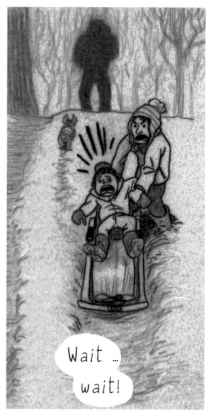

And another thing ... Every couple has pet names for each other, "baby" and stuff.

Now she just calls me by my first name and that bugs me.

Wait ...

wait!

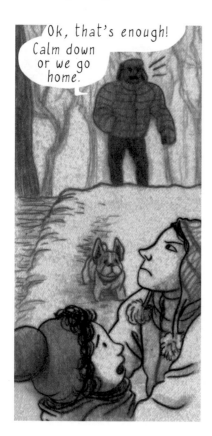

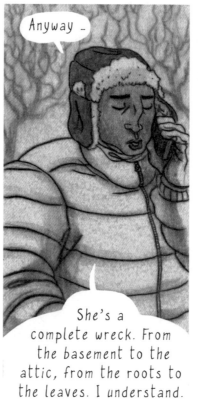

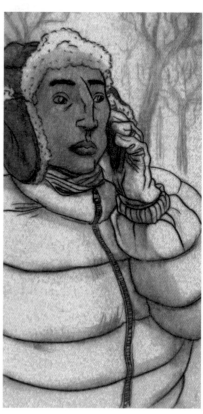

Ok, that's enough! Calm down or we go home.

Anyway ...

She's a complete wreck. From the basement to the attic, from the roots to the leaves. I understand.

Of course I'm staying! But I'm not staying for the kids, or because she's sick and might die soon. I'm staying because I love her. And because I understand her.

Ghost of Illness

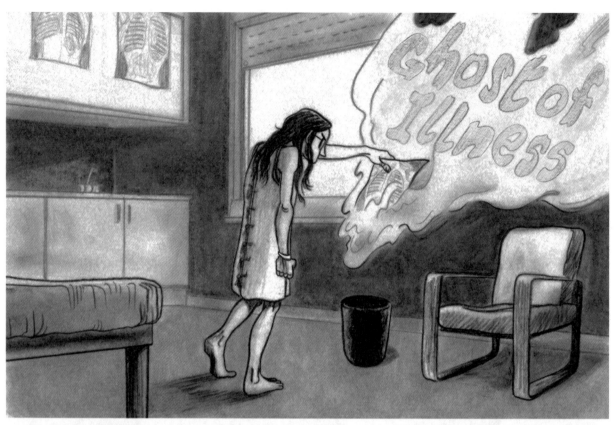

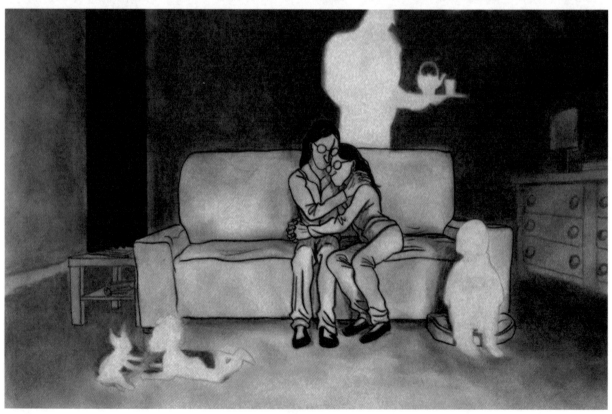

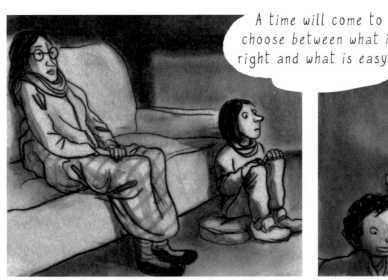

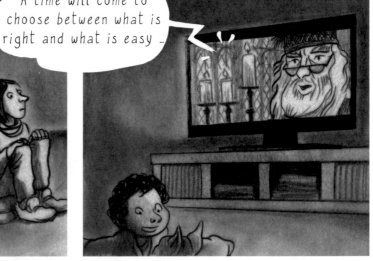

A time will come to choose between what is right and what is easy ...

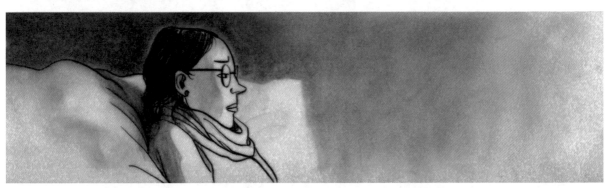

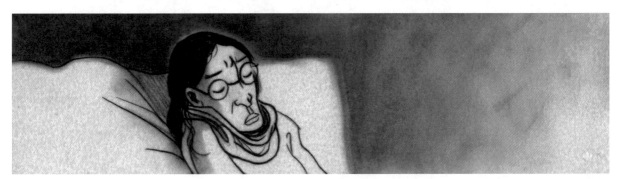

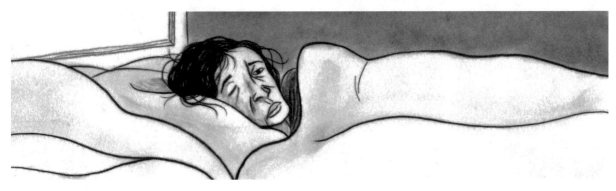

fff...
Every day that I open my eyes is a trial.
Oh, you're awake! Want some coffee now?
No, I feel sick from the pills.
Help me get up. If I could move, I'd break everything in sight.
You can break me without even touching me.
A bath?
A bath.

So, you see ... Everything is perfect in your relationship, except one very minor detail: monogamy.

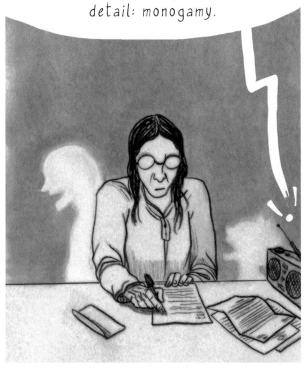

How many of us have found ourselves in this situation: we still love our partner but we're attracted by someone else ...

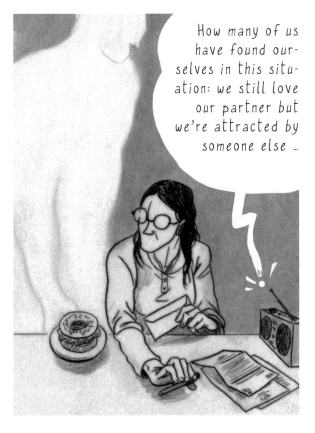

Because human relations are always changing. They're always moving and evolving.

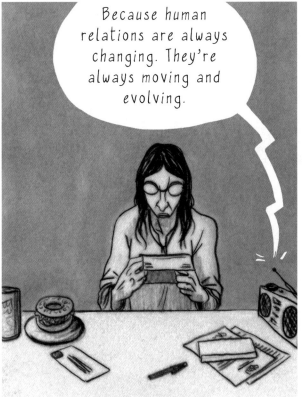

We expect certain things from them, we want them to be a certain way and lead us to certain results, whether it's marriage or an affair.

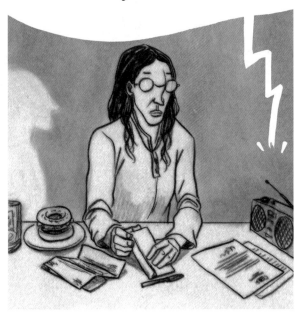

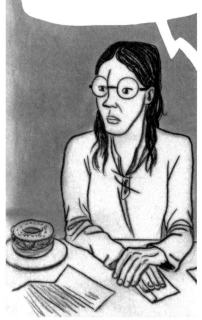

Let's accept the facts: we expect love to cure the frustrations and traumas in our lives.

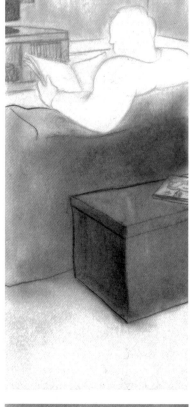

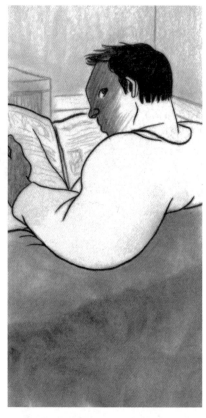

I know. Don't worry. Everything will work out.

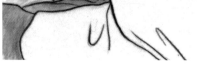

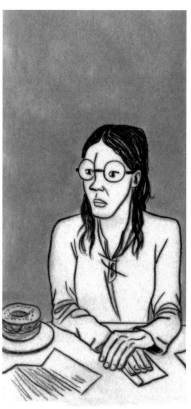

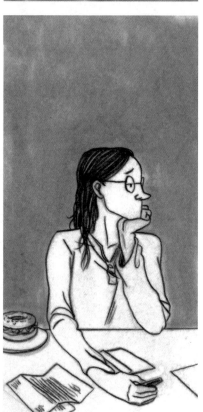

198

15.

REVELATION
UNDER ICE

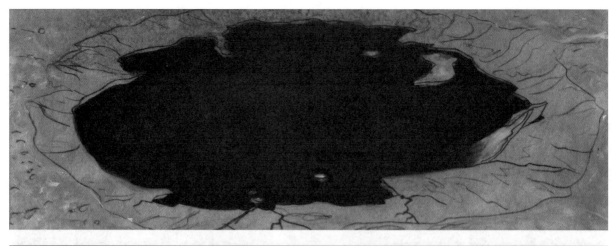

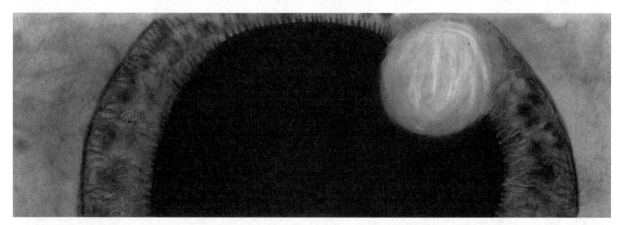

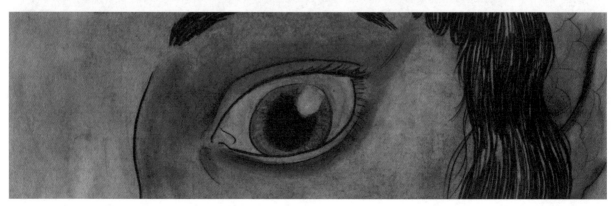

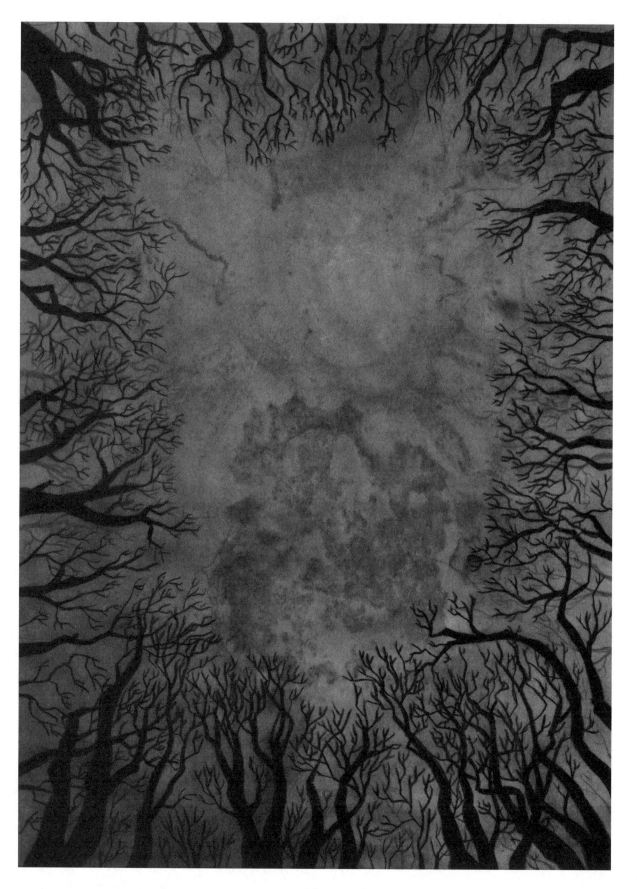

16.

In the Heat of the Club.
Saint Catherine Street East

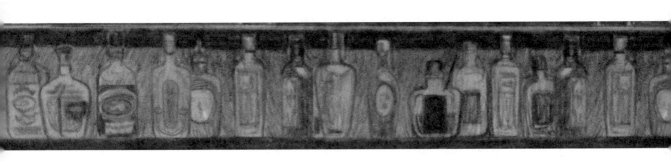

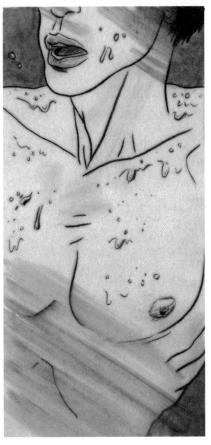

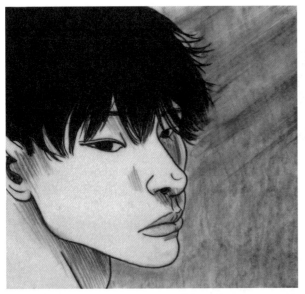
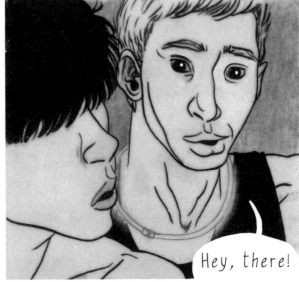

Hey, there!

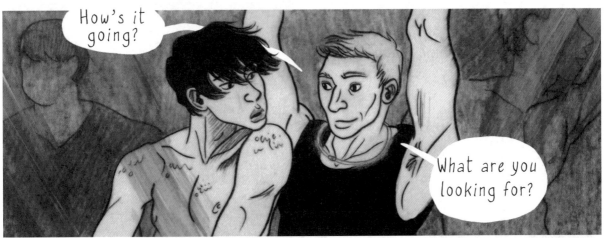

How's it going?

What are you looking for?

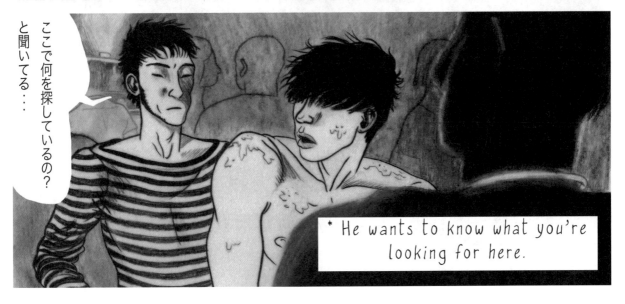

ここで何を探しているの？
と聞いてる…

* He wants to know what you're looking for here.

Oh, sorry, dude, are you tourists? Is this cutie with you?
Yes, he is with me.
踊りたい？
* Wanna dance?

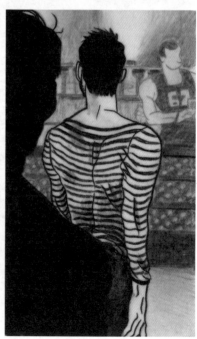

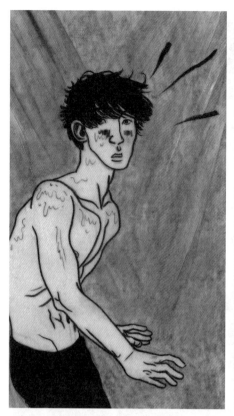
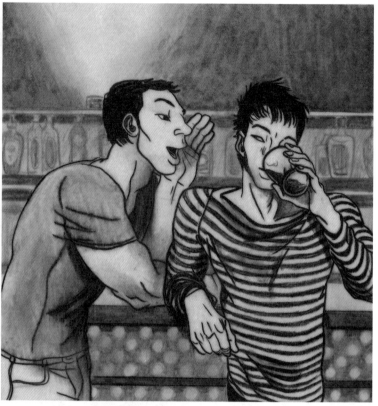
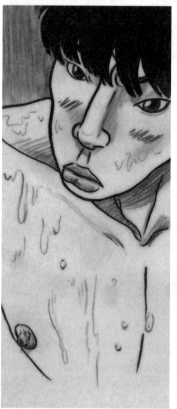
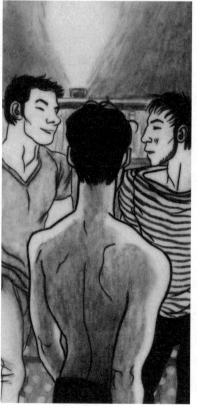
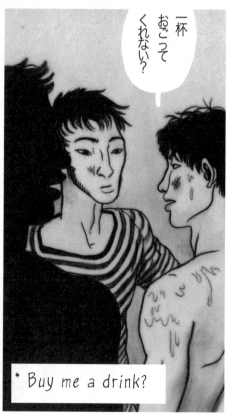

一杯
おごって
くれない？

* Buy me a drink?

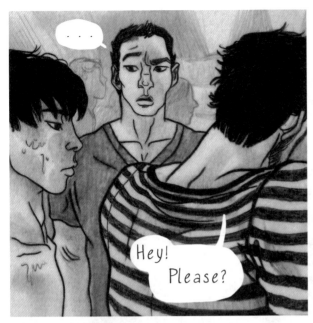

. . .

Hey! Please?

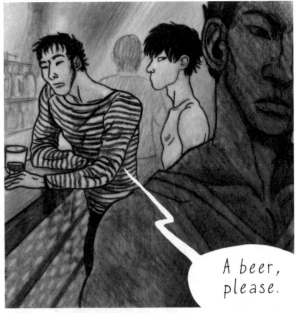

A beer, please.

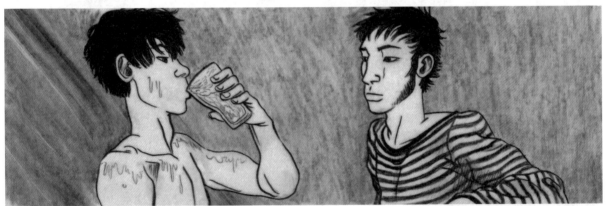

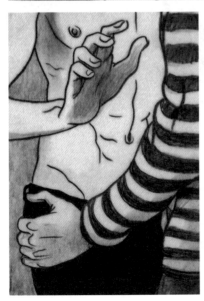

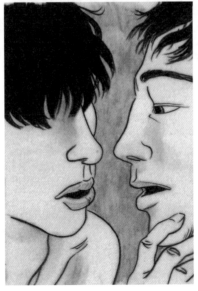

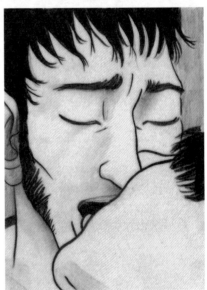

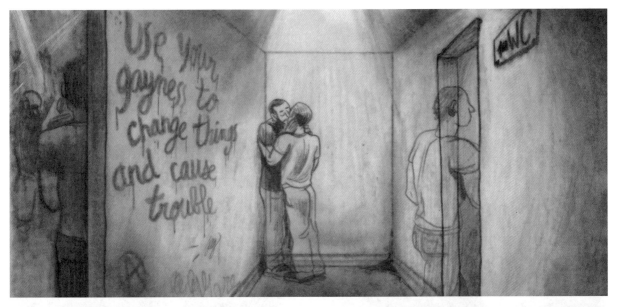

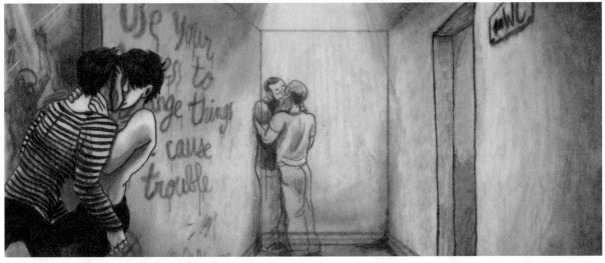

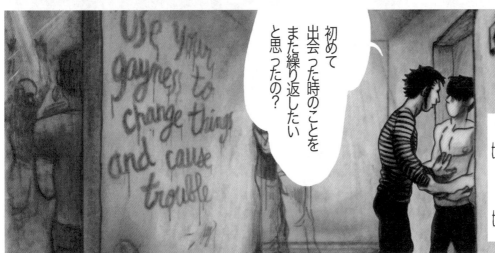

初めて出会った時のことをまた繰り返したいと思ったの？

* I thought the idea was to reenact the first time we met.

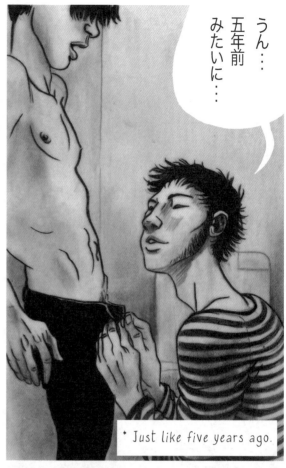

* Just like five years ago.

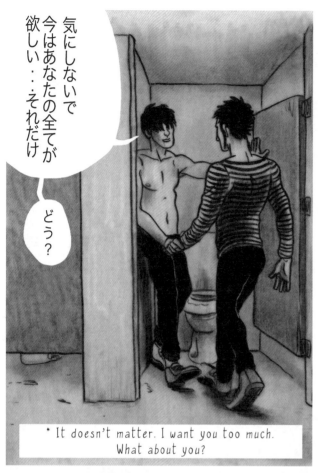

* It doesn't matter. I want you too much.
  What about you?

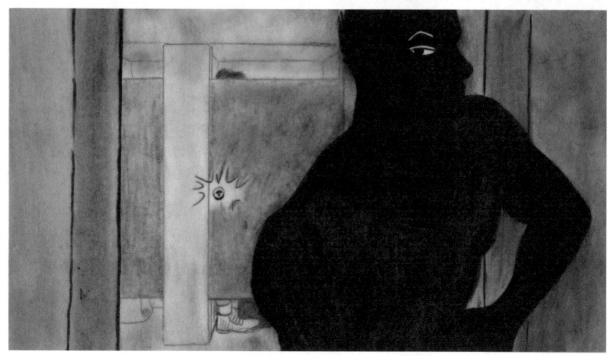

17.

Like a Ghost on My Retina

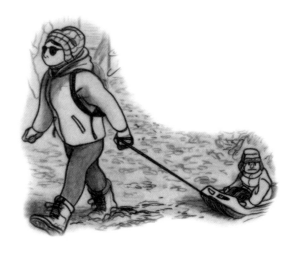

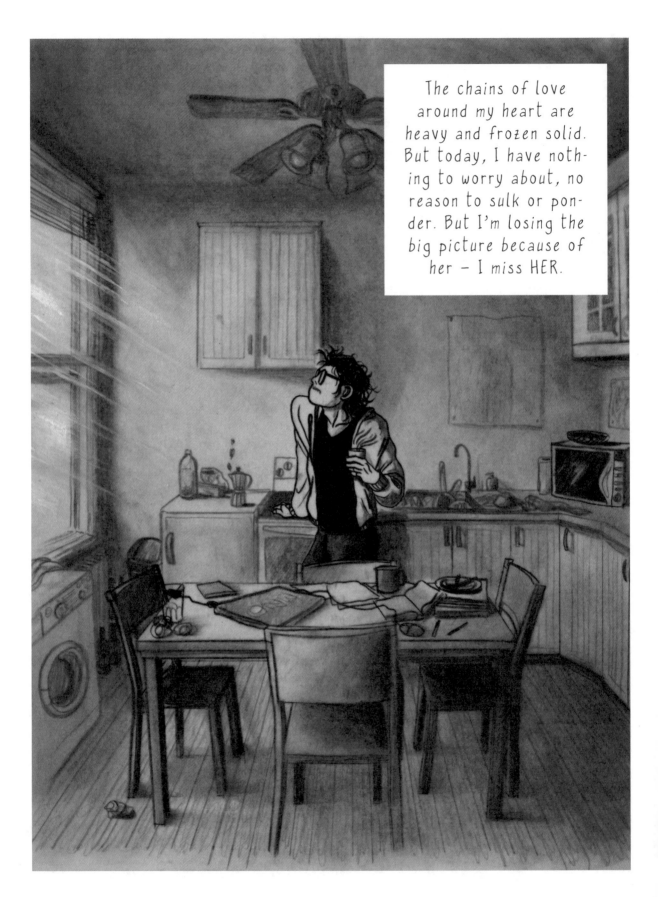

The chains of love around my heart are heavy and frozen solid. But today, I have nothing to worry about, no reason to sulk or ponder. But I'm losing the big picture because of her — I miss HER.

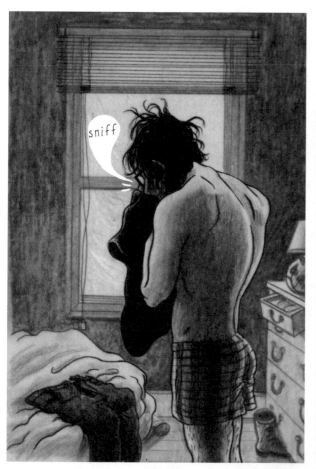

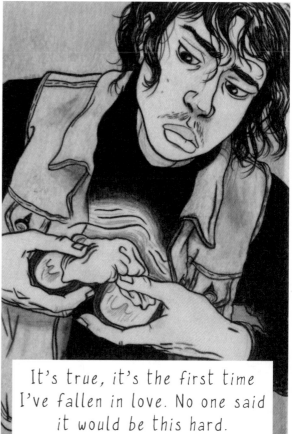

It's true, it's the first time I've fallen in love. No one said it would be this hard.

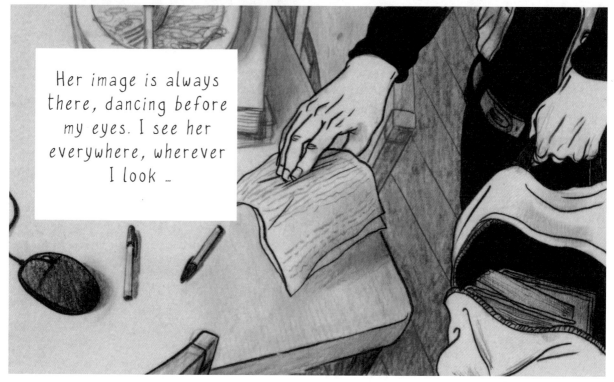

Her image is always there, dancing before my eyes. I see her everywhere, wherever I look …

Shit! No time to shovel the steps now!
I feel how distant she is, so I pretend I don't care, to see if she'll miss me too.

HEY! Wake up!
That's the technique. But what a stupid way to go about it!

VETEMENTS
JARRY

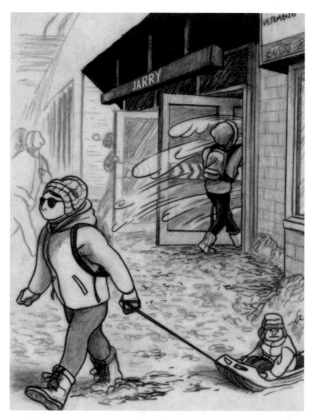

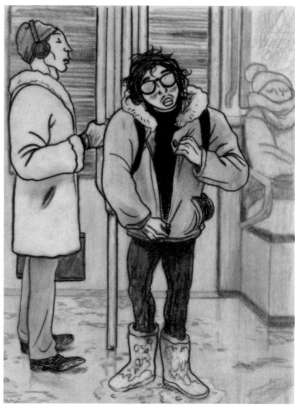

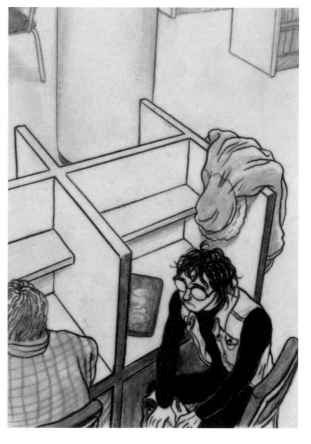

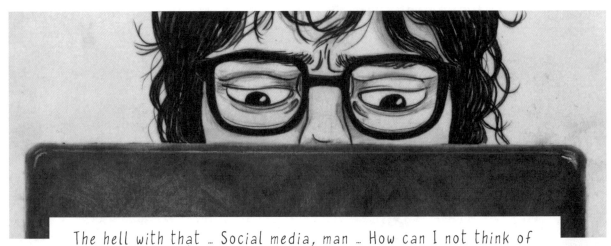

The hell with that ... Social media, man ... How can I not think of her? I'll see what she liked and what she posted, if she changed her photo or her profile, I'll stalk her on Twitter ... It's an invisible thread attached to my brain, pulling me in, night and day.

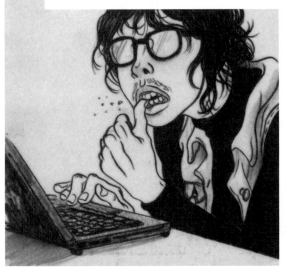

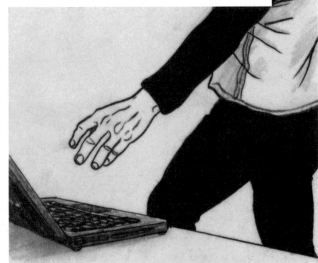

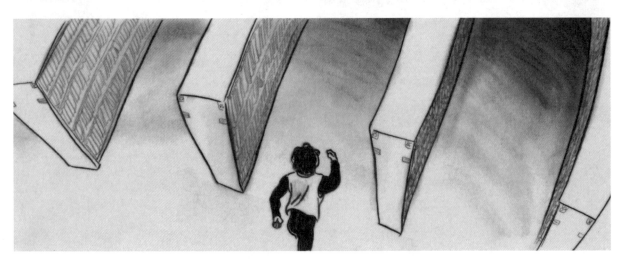

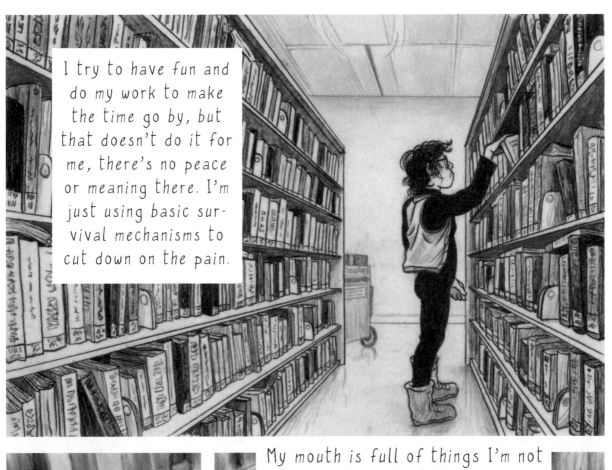

I try to have fun and do my work to make the time go by, but that doesn't do it for me, there's no peace or meaning there. I'm just using basic survival mechanisms to cut down on the pain.

My mouth is full of things I'm not allowed to tell her.

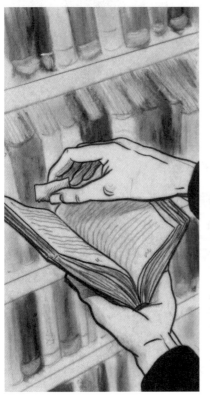

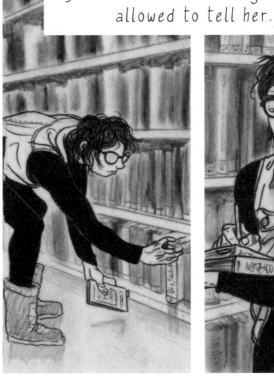

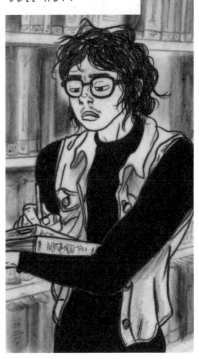

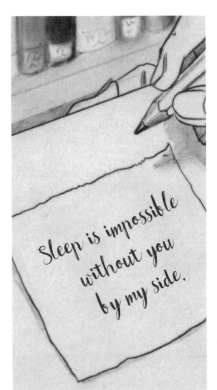

Sleep is impossible without you by my side.

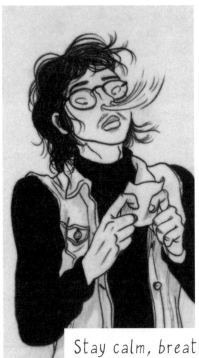

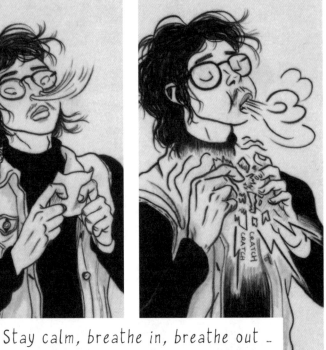

Stay calm, breathe in, breathe out ...

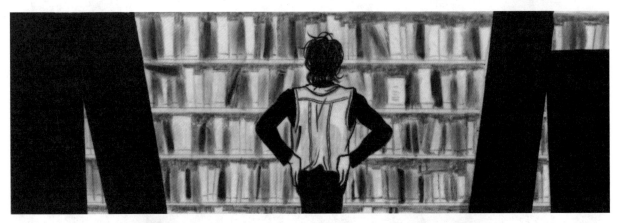

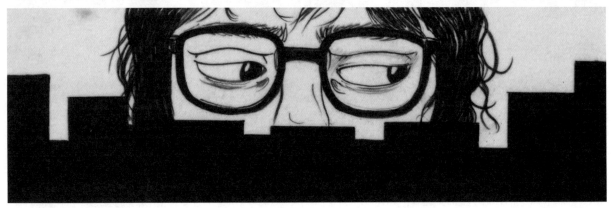

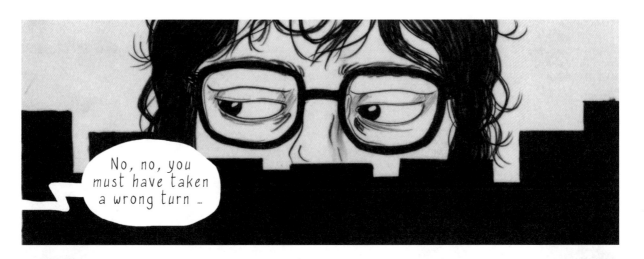

No, no, you must have taken a wrong turn …

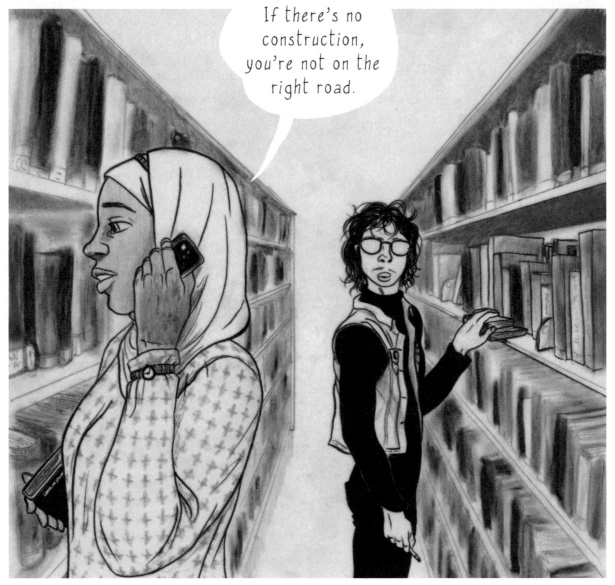

If there's no construction, you're not on the right road.

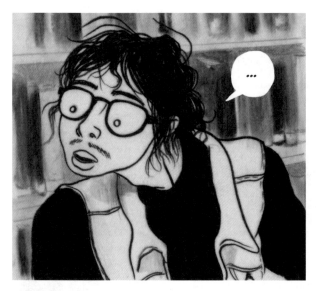

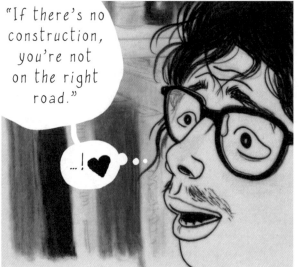

"If there's no construction, you're not on the right road."

...

...! ♥ ...

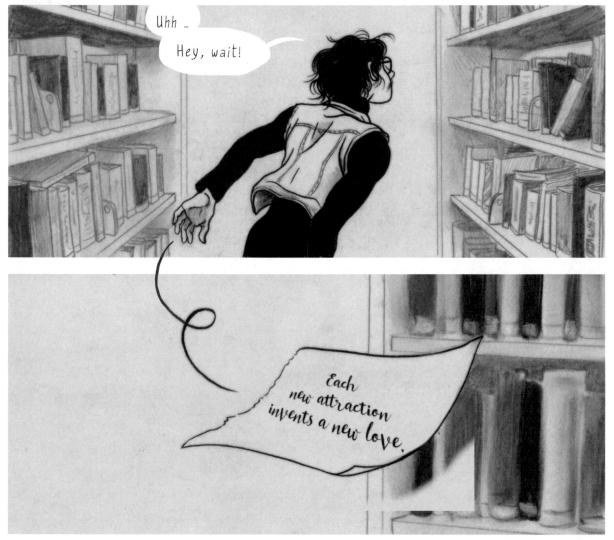

Uhh ...
Hey, wait!

Each new attraction invents a new love.

18.

On the Importance of Laughter

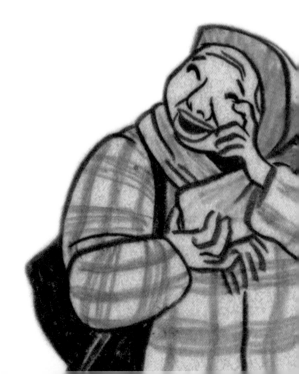

Isn't it getting a little boring? Won't it ever end?
What?
Winter, of course! What else?
Le Dépanneur Café
ESPRESSO
DEJEUNERS
MUSIQUE LIVE TOUS LES JOURS

The only natural thing they have here in Canada is maple syrup!
What a place!
Can't wait to go home! Give me a good goat cheese.
HA HA HA HA
Damned European colonizers! Now where did I park my car?
I'll get some bagels, then I'll drive you home.
ST VIATEUR
BAGEL

Hello? Yes, yes, that's me ... Yes.
I ... WHAT?
Oh, boy, now what happened?
Mom, listen...

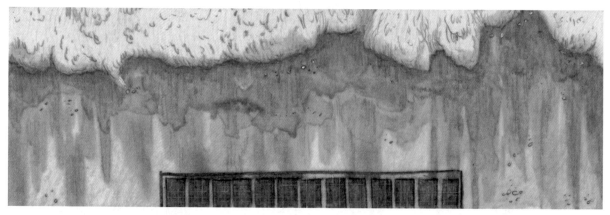

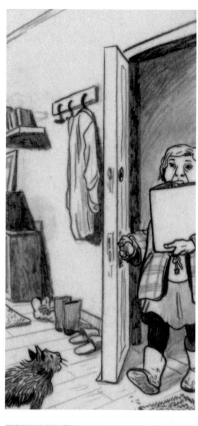
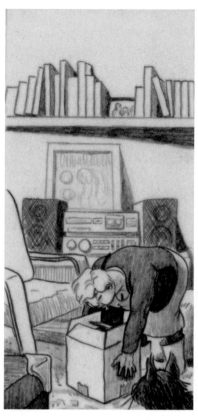
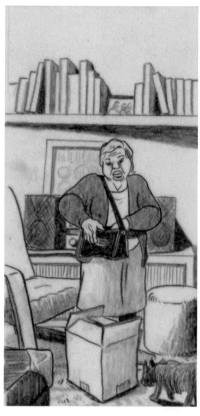
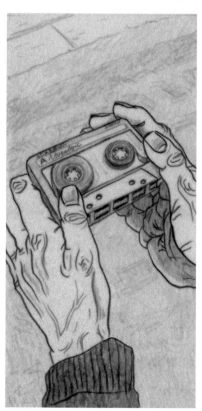
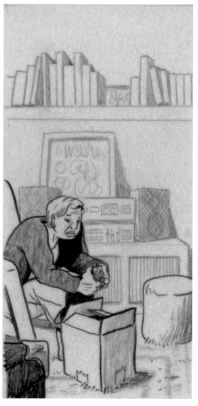
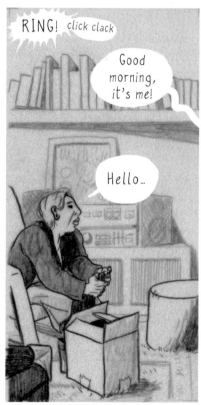

RING! *click clack*

Good morning, it's me!

Hello…

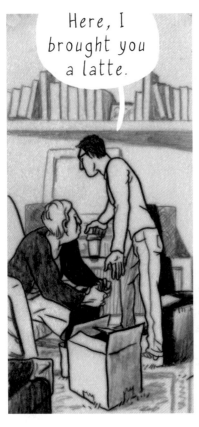

Here, I brought you a latte.

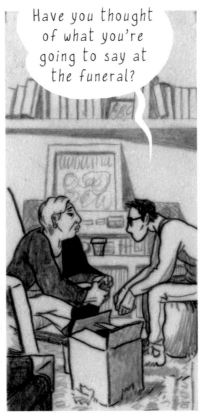

Have you thought of what you're going to say at the funeral?

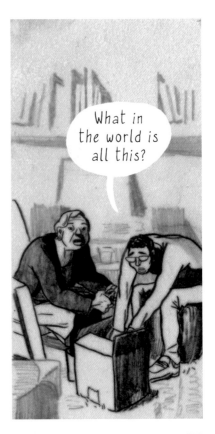

What *in* the world is all this?

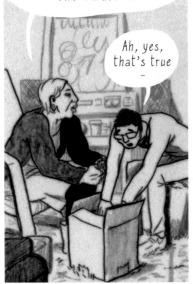

You know your father loved collecting audio cassettes. He made play-lists for every occasion, and recorded pieces off the radio …

Ah, yes, that's true …

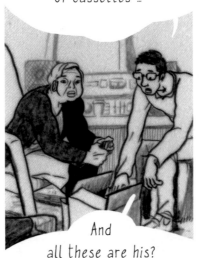

The last one he gave me was for my graduation. But then CDs got popular … and there was that fight we had in 2001 and we stopped speaking. I'd forgotten all about his love of cassettes …

And all these are his?

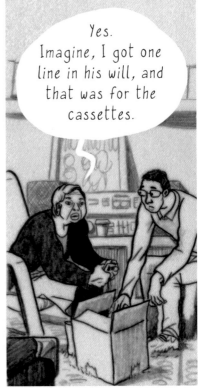

Yes. Imagine, I got one line in his will, and that was for the cassettes.

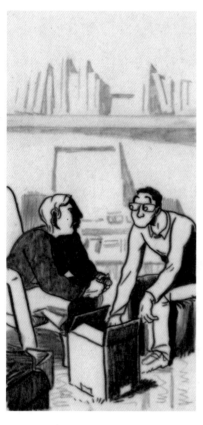

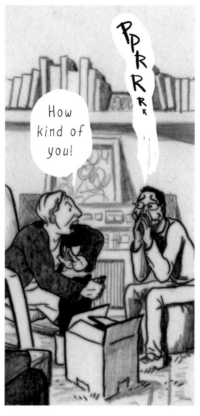

How kind of you!

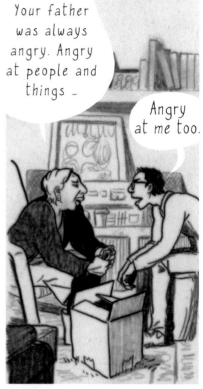

Your father was always angry. Angry at people and things …

Angry at me too.

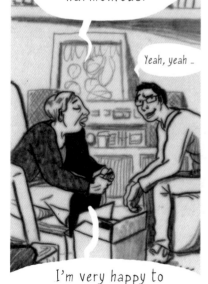

And at me when I left, but when we were together and in love, our life was perfectly harmonious.

Yeah, yeah …

I'm very happy to have these cassettes …

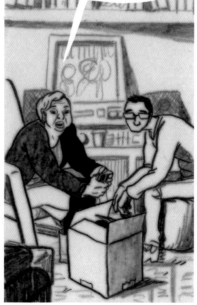

They're the soundtrack of our life together. And a big part of my life, certainly the best part.

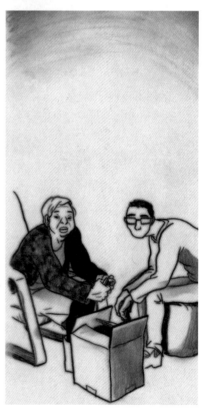

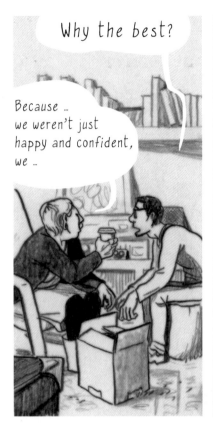

Why the best?

Because ...
we weren't just
happy and confident,
we ...

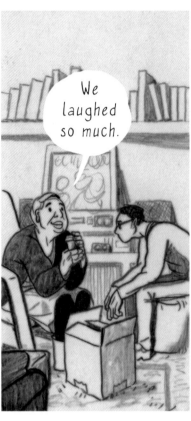

We
laughed
so much.

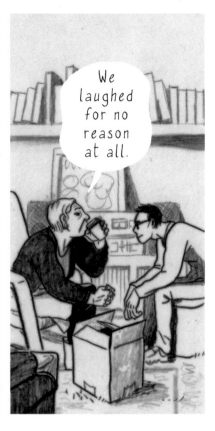

We
laughed
for no
reason
at all.

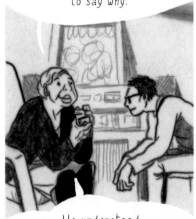

Something would happen, and we'd
look at each other ... We'd just burst
out laughing without having
to say why.

We understood
we were seeing the same thing,
and we'd just start laughing,
just like that ...

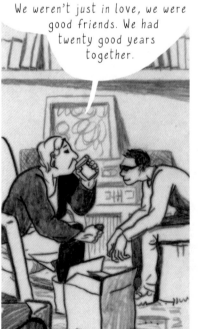

We weren't just in love, we were
good friends. We had
twenty good years
together.

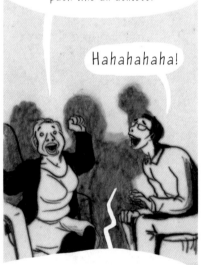

Oh boy, I laughed so much I had a six-
pack like an athlete!

Hahahahaha!

Come on, you'd had me, I'm sure
the laughter was good, but you
were no Venus Williams!

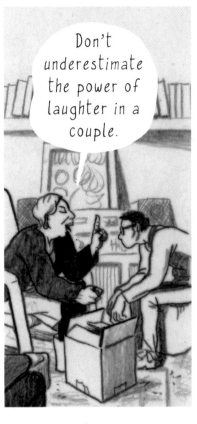

Don't underestimate the power of laughter in a couple.

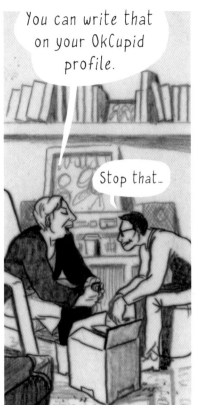

You can write that on your OkCupid profile.

Stop that…

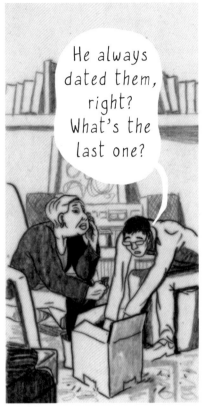

He always dated them, right? What's the last one?

This one, I'm sure. It was in the car's sound system when …

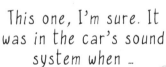

They … they were able to fish out the cassette?

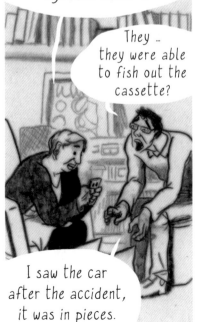

I saw the car after the accident, it was in pieces.

Your father too … We're such fragile things. We've built the pyramids, designed rockets, painted the Mona Lisa, lit up cities …

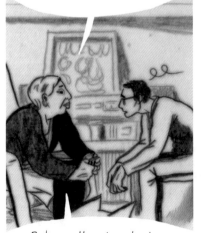

But we all end up broken, while such a puny little object survives …

See, the tape stopped playing when the crash happened, in the middle of a song, I bet …

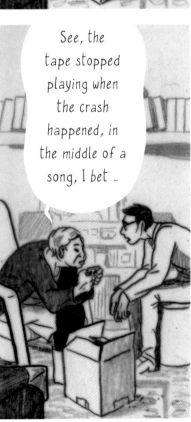

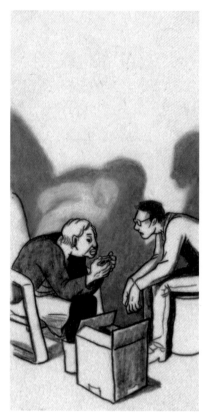

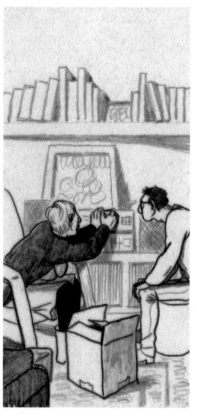

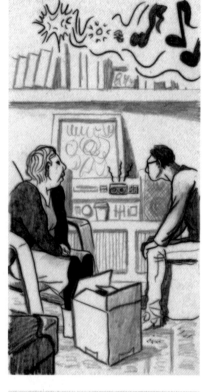

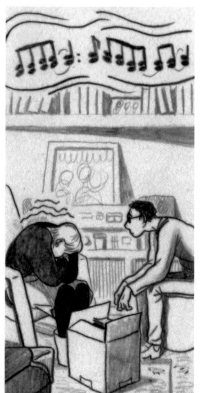

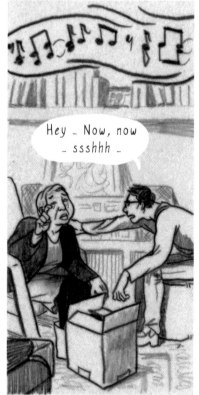

Hey ... Now, now ... ssshhh ...

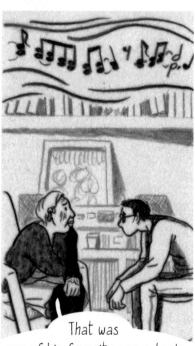

That was one of his favorite songs back then. He'd sing it to wake me up in the morning.

You okay?
Yes, yes ...
Life is cruel and ironic. We have to crush it with our dancing feet.
And with songs like this one.

You'll see, life involves a lot of mourning.
I don't get it.
Mourning means doing what you used to do with someone else, only alone now.
I hope I'll get to laugh as much as you did.
Stop!

19.

On Mount Royal:
Our Lives Together

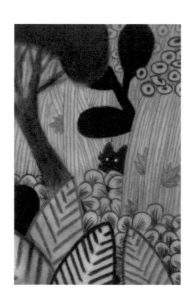

Squeak
Squee
Creak
Creak
Squee
Squeak

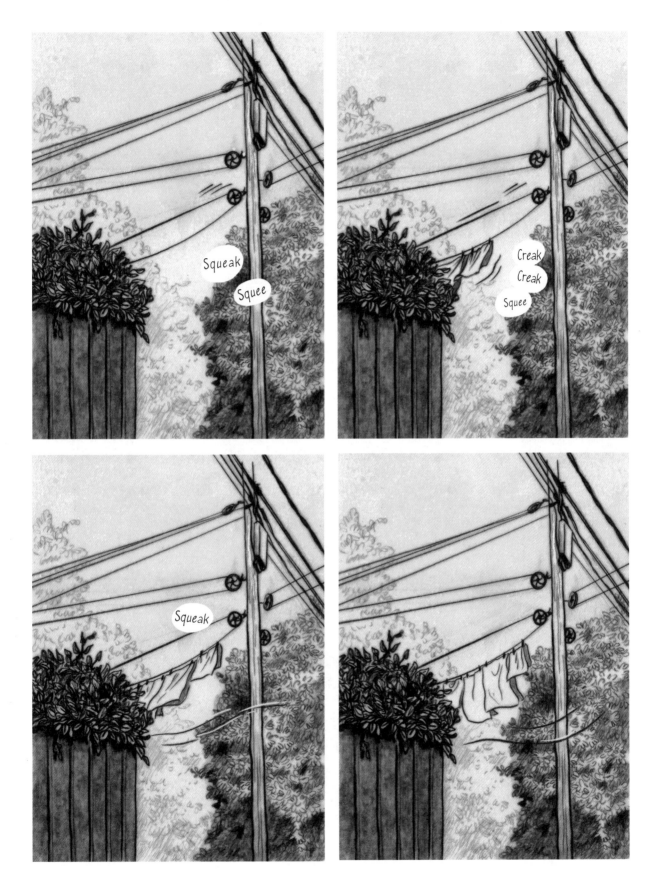

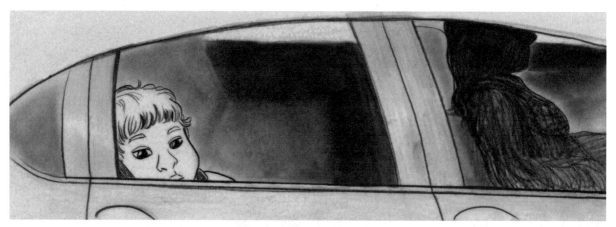

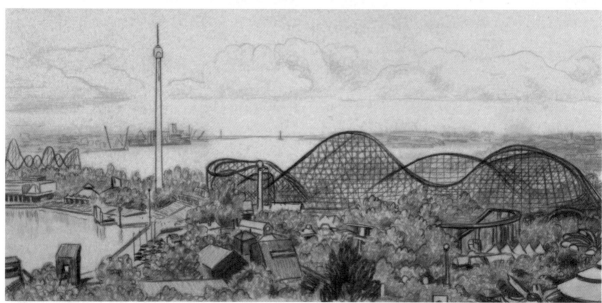

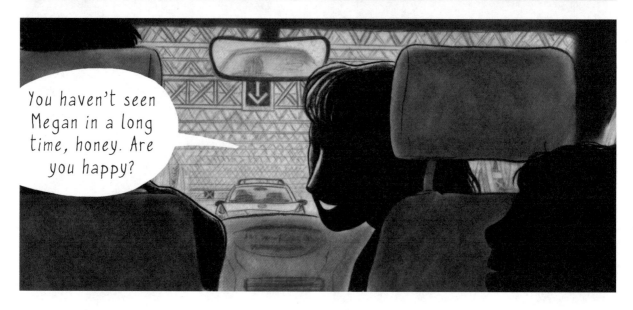

You haven't seen Megan in a long time, honey. Are you happy?

Of course!

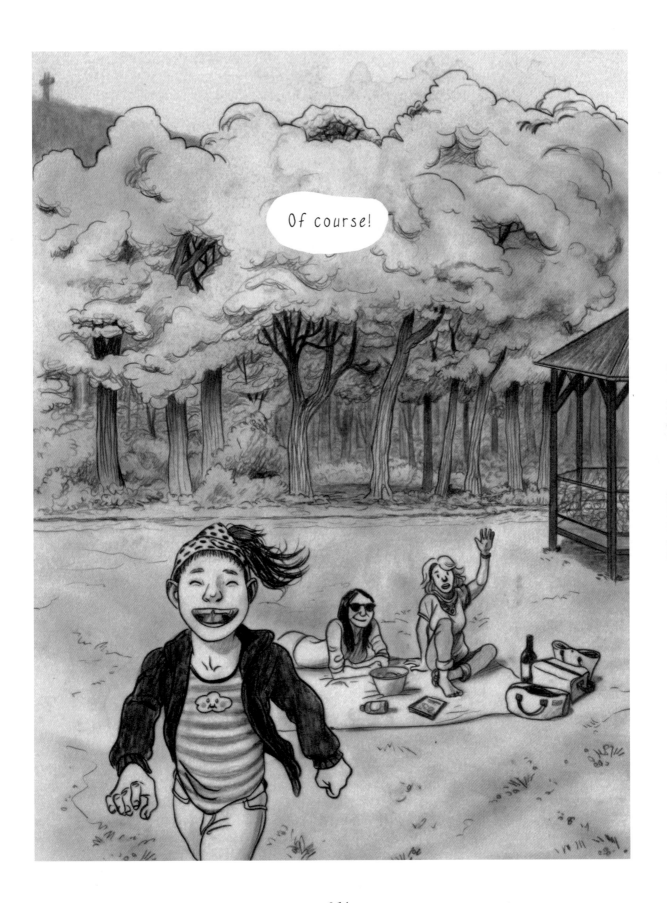

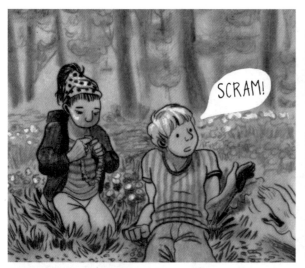

SCRAM!

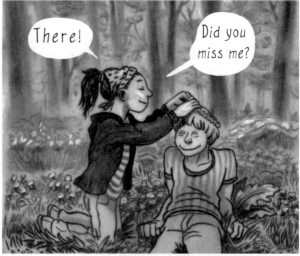

There!

Did you miss me?

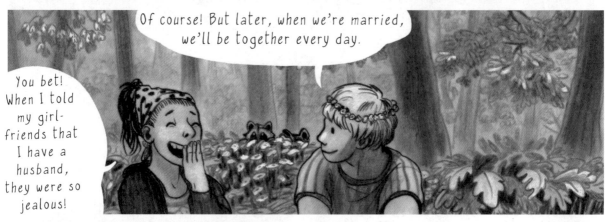

Of course! But later, when we're married, we'll be together every day.

You bet! When I told my girl-friends that I have a husband, they were so jealous!

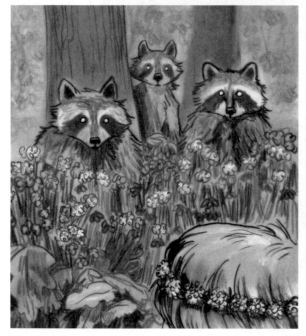

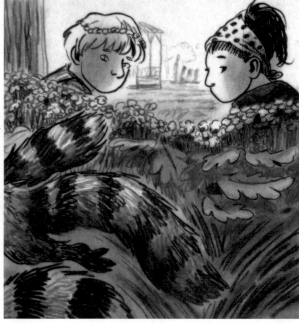

But … I don't know *if* I want to be a boy …

I'm supposed to be tough because I'm a boy, and fight, and not cry and all the rest …

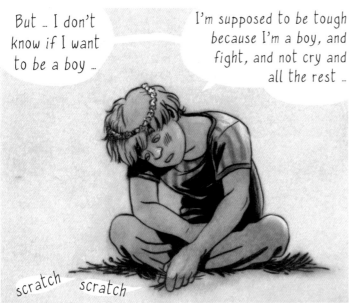

scratch   scratch

Would you be with me if I was a girl?

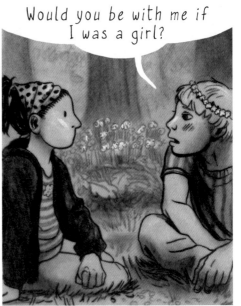

We could buy clothes together … And try them on in the same fitting room in the store …

And wear each other's shoes at the house …

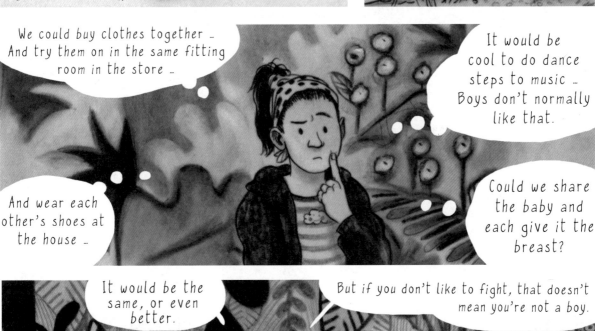

It would be cool to do dance steps to music … Boys don't normally like that.

Could we share the baby and each give it the breast?

It would be the same, or even better.

But if you don't like to fight, that doesn't mean you're not a boy.

Hmm…

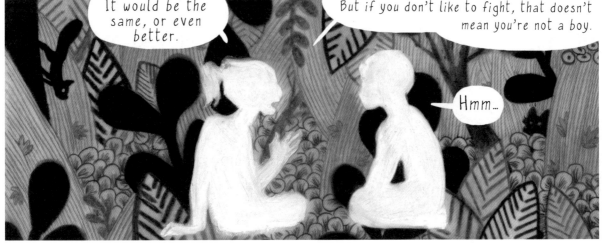

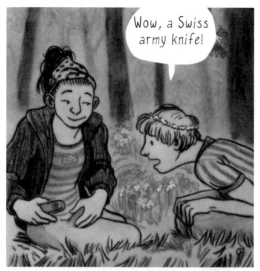

Wow, a Swiss army knife!

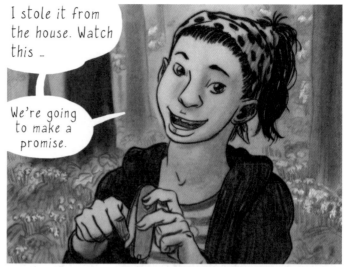

I stole it from the house. Watch this ...

We're going to make a promise.

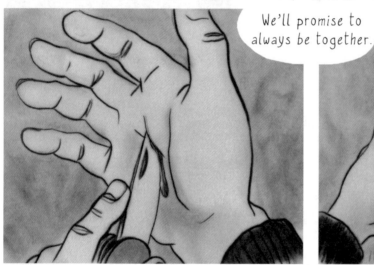

We'll promise to always be together.

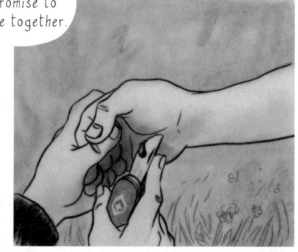

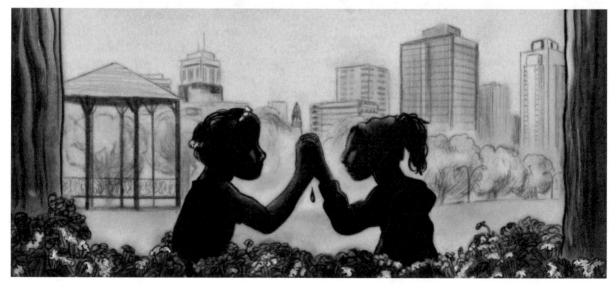

M+S
From now on, nothing will keep us apart.

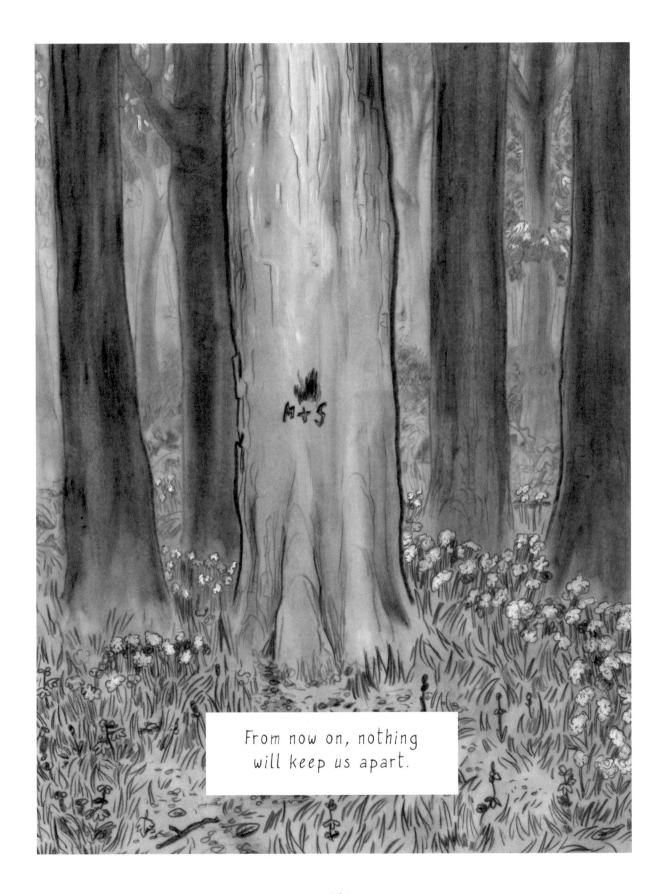

20.

Togetherness
with a Capital T

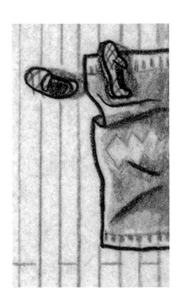

Meow
Mee!
Ow!
Please, go feed the cat.
Mew?
It's your cat, it was your birthday present.
It was your idea.
MEOW

You wanted children. I gave you three who fortunately turned into three grown-up men who leave us alone now that they have their condo.
Meow
So you feed the cat.
Ha! If we started counting things from the last thirty years, you'd feed the cat every day AND clean out the litter box!
Pfff!
Mew.
Purr.
I love you.
Yeah, yeah, I love you too. Look, I got up.
Purr
Purrrr
Sniff Sniff

JESUS CHRIST! You farted on purpose before you got up!!
HA HA HA HA!

21.

The Aftermath
(Epilogue)

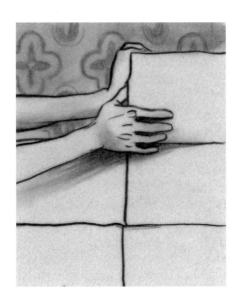

Wait for meeee!

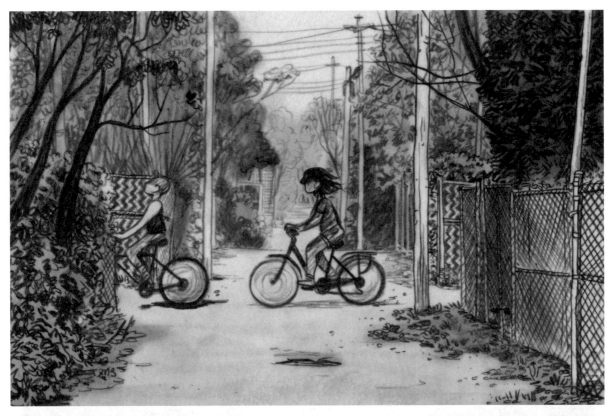

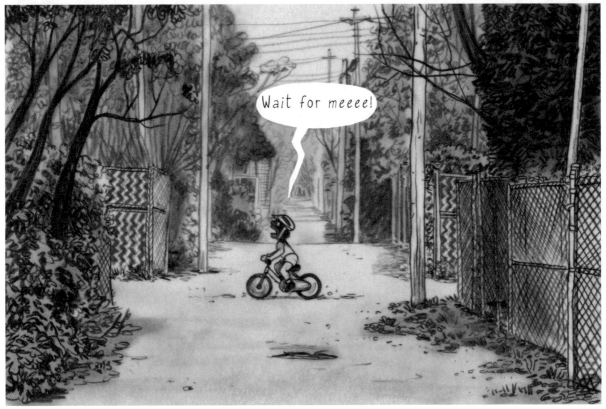

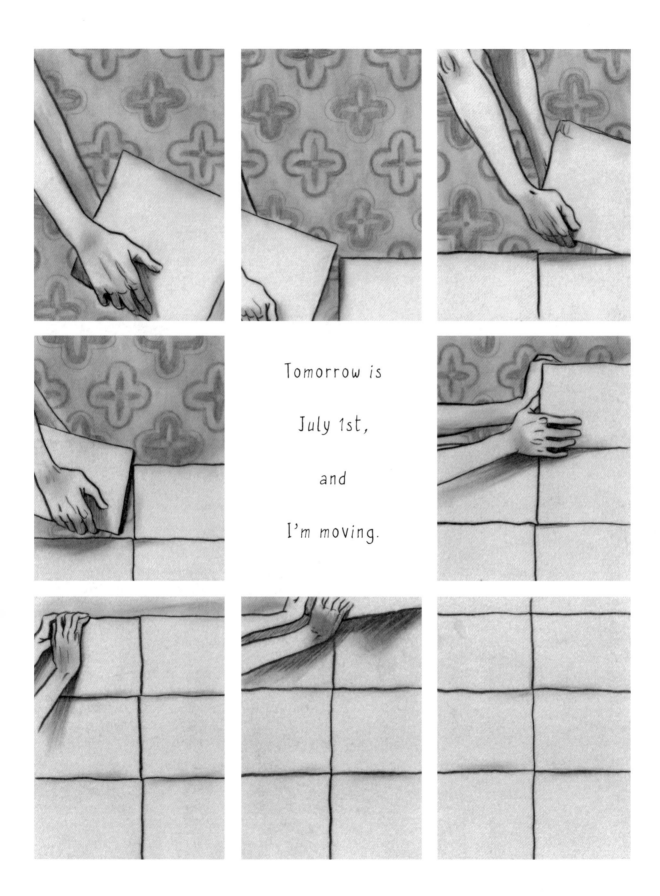

Tomorrow is

July 1st,

and

I'm moving.

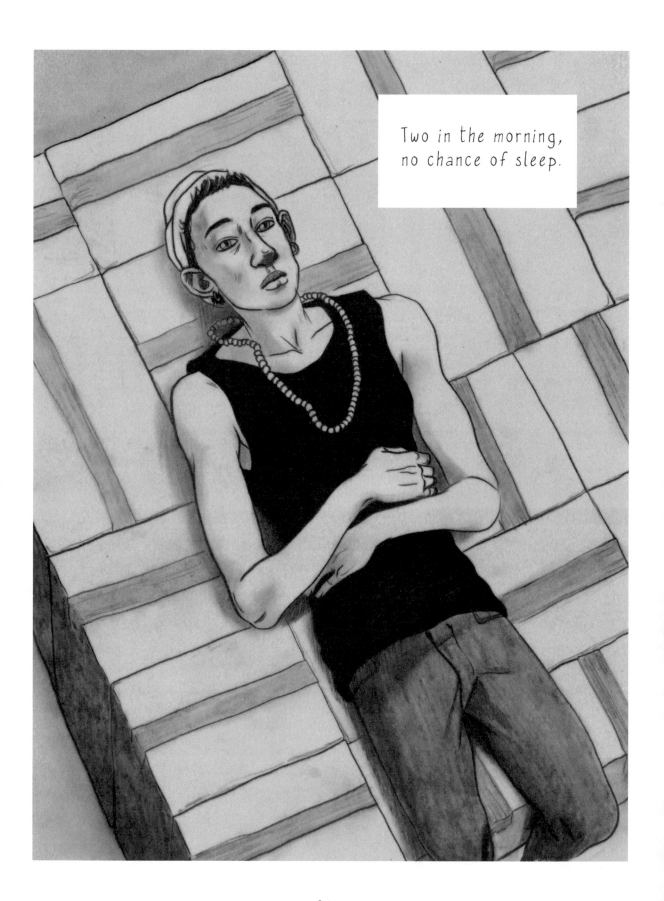

Two in the morning,
no chance of sleep.

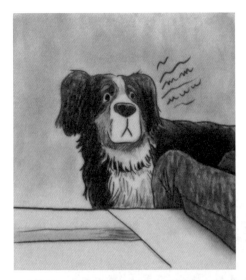

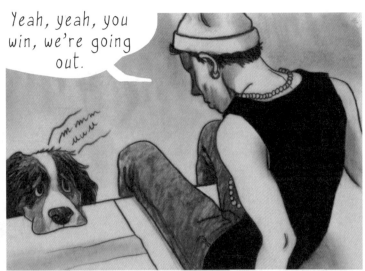

Yeah, yeah, you win, we're going out.

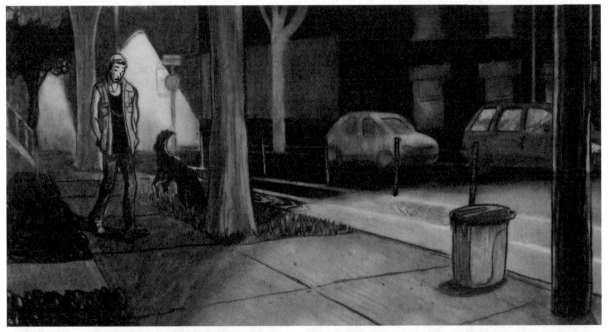

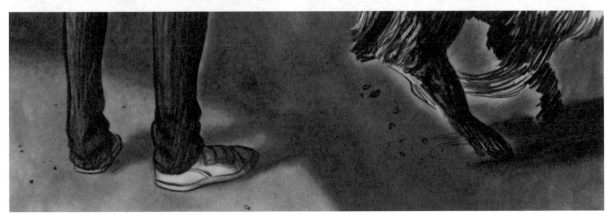

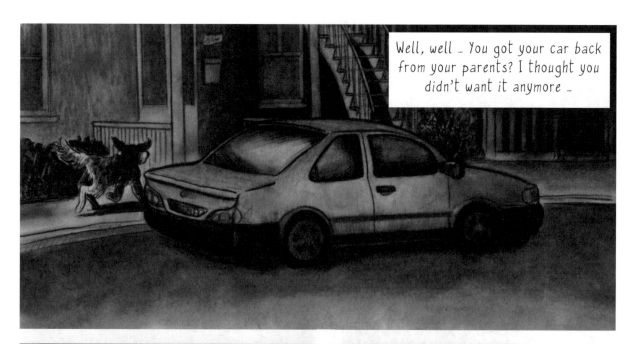

Well, well ... You got your car back from your parents? I thought you didn't want it anymore ...

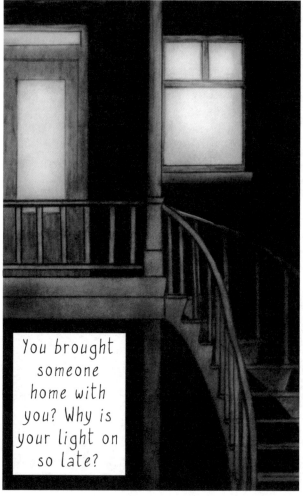

You brought someone home with you? Why is your light on so late?

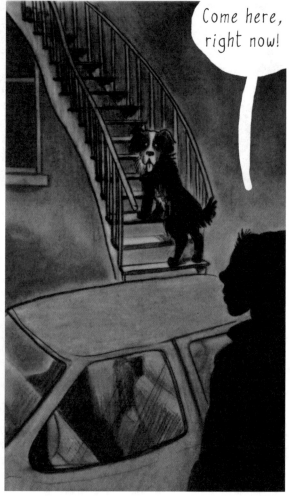

Come here, right now!

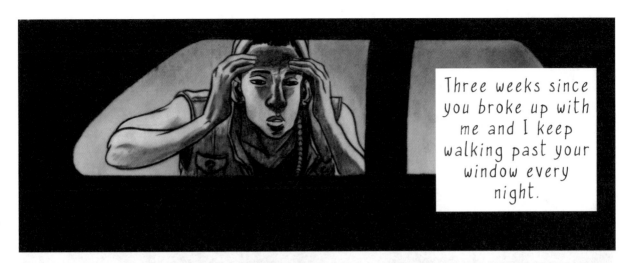

Three weeks since you broke up with me and I keep walking past your window every night.

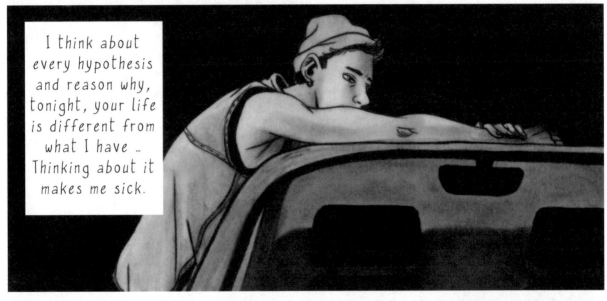

I think about every hypothesis and reason why, tonight, your life is different from what I have ... Thinking about it makes me sick.

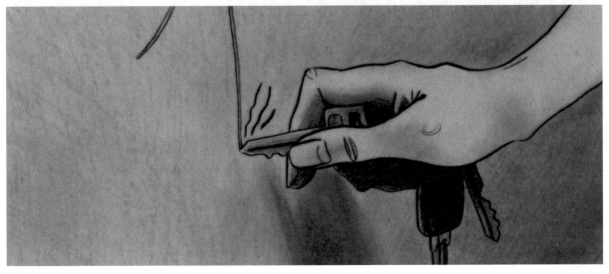

How can I shrug off the hold you have over me?
My brain can't be rational.
My lungs refuse to breathe in the facts.
My heart awaits.
My belly calls out.

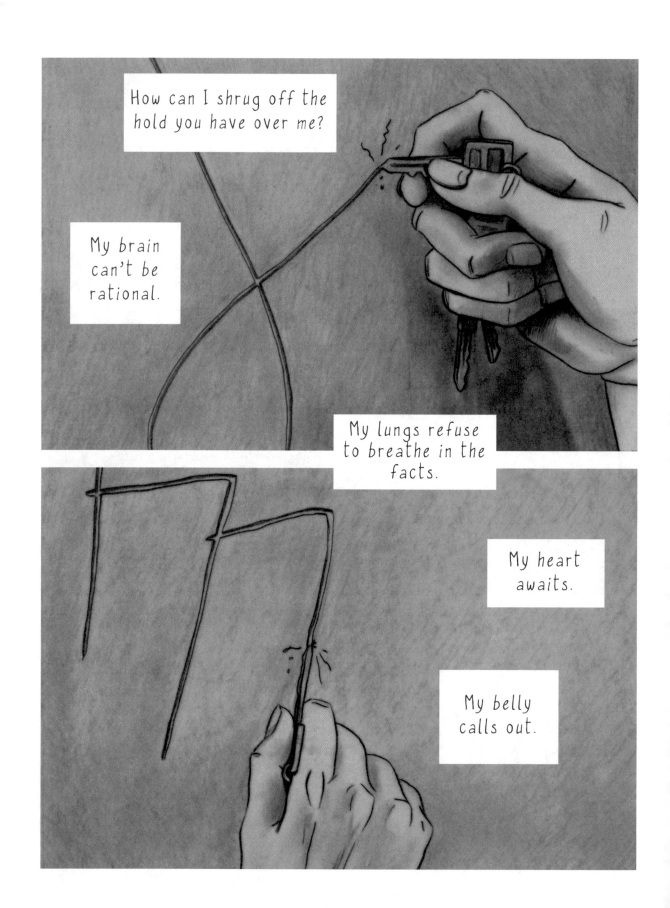

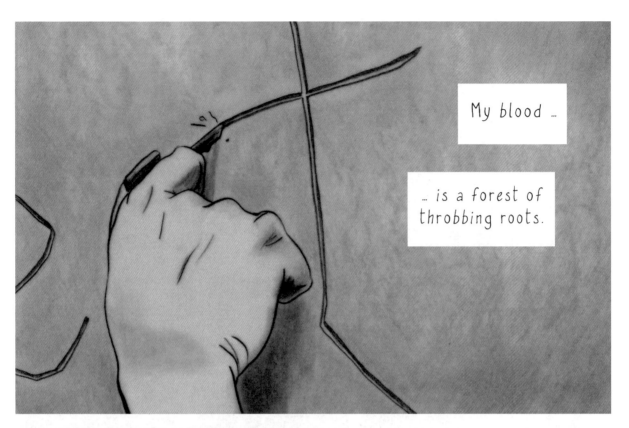

My blood ...

... is a forest of throbbing roots.

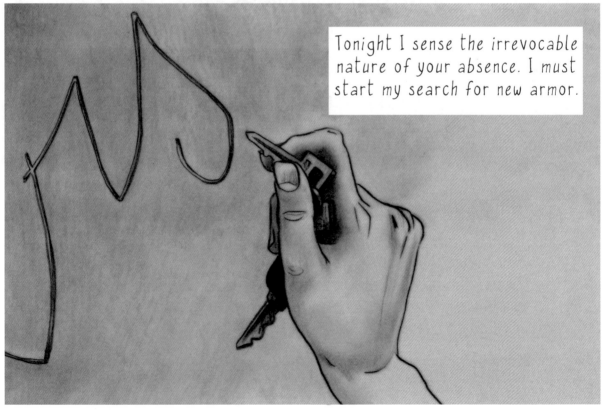

Tonight I sense the irrevocable nature of your absence. I must start my search for new armor.

I still love you

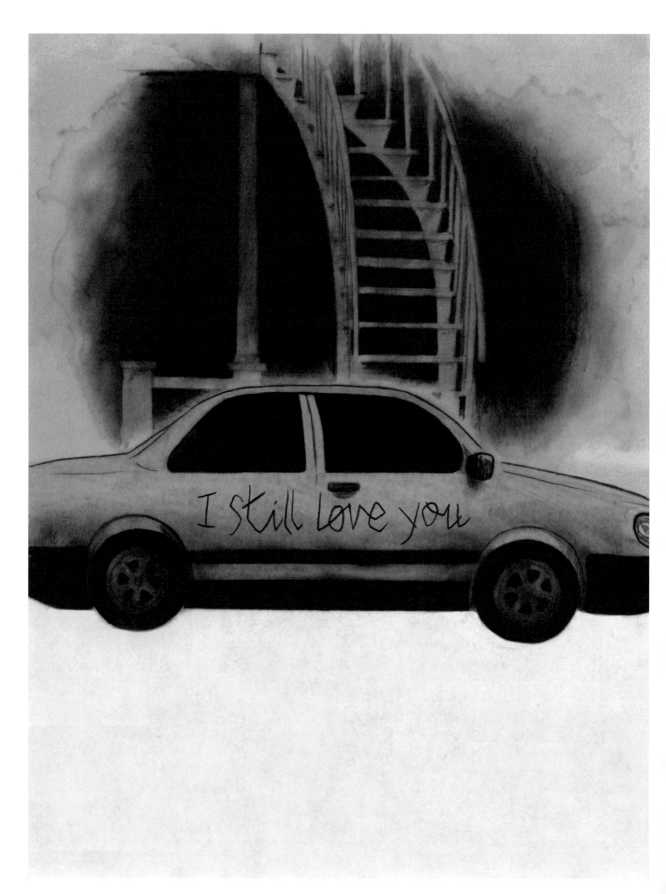

For their reading, their good advice, the shelter they offered,
my thanks go to:

Baptiste Amsallem, Jimmy Beaulieu, David Benito, CÄät, Ceh-
seel & Alex, Lorenzo Chiavini & his family as well as Irma, Virginie
Despentes, Viva Dirm & Miriam Ginestier, Elric Dufau, Alexandre Fon-
taine Rousseau & Cathon, Marianne Gauthier, Benoît Guillaume, the
Jouvray-Ollagnier family, Mathilde Laurier, Lisa Mandel, Chloé Mazlo,
Maya Mihindou, the Piccinini-Varrà family, Johanna Schipper, Susanna Scrivo, Carole Stromboni, Nolwenn Trillot, Claire Valageas.

Thanks to the staff at Glénat, always welcoming and ready to listen.

A shout-out to my Montreal friends at the 7070, and the afternoons
at Laurier Park.

For all the hours of the day and night spent speaking of love, a special shout-out to my sisters and brothers who know who they are.

For all the winds that carried her to me and for all her support, my
last thought is for Susanna.

—Julie Maroh

Also by Julie Maroh:

Blue Is the Warmest Color (2013)

Skandalon (2014)

For more info:

juliemaroh.com